EVERYMAN'S GUIDE TO ORGASM

(The Dark Side of Sex in America)

EVERYMAN'S GUIDE TO ORGASM

(The Dark Side of Sex in America)

Reflections of a Divorce Lawyer

Raymond A. Macdonald

ISBN: 1537691465
ISBN 13: 9781537691466
Library of Congress Control Number: TXu001705916 / 2009-08-11

Contents

CHAPTER 1
Always, Never, Sometimes

n 2005 the *New York Times* ran an article informing readers that one-third of American women experienced regular orgasm, one-third never had the experience, and one-third were in the sometimes category.[1] This came as a shock to me. It was as if living in the sixteenth century I had just learned of Copernicus's discovery that the earth was not the center of the universe, that instead the planets—including the earth—revolved around the sun, and not the reverse.

Do not misunderstand. It was not that as a divorce lawyer, with several decades of experience in domestic strife or as a divorced man myself searching for a mate, I was unaware that some such distribution of female responsiveness was one of the principal causes of the continuing battle of the sexes, or the cause of a large percentage of divorces I handled. It was just having it laid out with such diagrammatic neatness that it struck me for the first time that in reality there was not one gender called "woman" to consider. There are three separate subspecies, as different in their thoughts, habit, desires, and antipathies, as say a German shepherd is from a Pekingese, or a chimpanzee from a Bonobo.

My experience as a divorce lawyer, as well as personal love-life or absence thereof, plus news and stories of mayhem and murder between the sexes, stories that are misleadingly called "factual" and distinguished from what is equally misleadingly called "fictional" suddenly fell into place. Even what seemed to be purely factual observations about women, such as those of the promiscuous Don Juan or the short story writer, Guy de Maupassant, suddenly seemed in need of revaluation.

Readers probably do not recall the section on de Maupassant in the famous or infamous *My Life and Loves*, written by Frank Harris.[2] In that book, the eponymous author's principle object in visiting the French writer was to confirm or deny the story of his almost absolute control over the behavior of what Marlon Brando called his "noble tool." Harris relates that he was astounded when de Maupassant demonstrated his ability to call his member to attention, and have it remain in that position on command. This is not what I wish to recall, however.

Harris was disappointed on hearing de Maupassant assert that of the hundred or more "conquests" in the last year or so, most were not especially passionate. In fact, most women he experienced were "cool." And so, he opined, it was doubtless with the whole sex. This was a cardinal disappointment to read. And he was speaking of French women! It seemed even worse than one's personal experiences would lead one to believe. Nonetheless, when I read Harris's report, I accepted it with some dismay at more or less face value.

But that was before I discovered the *New York Times* taxonomy! It was also before I had several years of personal experience. Now, reconsidering de Maupassant's evaluation of the coolness of the opposite sex, I realized that the follow-up questions should have been, where did the French writer find this battalion of willing women he boasted of having, and more importantly, in which of the three taxonomic subspecies should they be placed?

Once the question is asked, the answer emerges almost automatically. The greatest number was doubtless promiscuous groupies or prostitutes or women on the rebound, all of them, almost by definition, sexually disturbed. In other words, de Maupassant's evaluation of the opposite sex was probably based almost exclusively on experiences he had had with only one type of woman, as categorized by the *NYT's* taxonomy, the inorgasmic woman.

Thank you, *New York Times*! If your reportage on politics, international relations, and military campaigns were as informative, the *Times* might without radical hypocrisy claim to report "All the News That's Fit to Print." What struck me, as a divorce lawyer, was that it was simply excessively general to consider "women" as one gender. Three essentially different and distinct subspecies must be identified and considered if one is to fully understand the complaints and controversies of husbands and wives, the causes of divorce and the many legal as well as nonlegal misunderstandings and disasters, private and public, which result from ignorance of dissatisfactions originating in the bedroom.

CHAPTER 2
Three Hollywood Love Goddesses

thought of my own history of wrongheaded estimates while sitting in a movie theater some years ago, and viewing Ava Gardner, who was considered one of the sexiest actresses alive. No one compared to her. I saw her in the 1949 movie *The Bribe*, in which her hushed voice and the soft focus lens made her seem a virtual goddess.[1] I was enraptured. It took several hours for my overheated brain and other body parts to descend to normal.

Recently, I was delighted to learn that author and painter Henry Miller thought she was the sexiest female he had ever seen.[2] For her part, she kept a print he sent her of his watercolor, *Three Heads*, signed and inscribed to Divine Ava which hung in her London residence for many years.[3]

Now equipped with this *New York Times* taxonomy, I took another look at the 1957 film based on Ernest Hemingway's book, *The Sun Also Rises*.[4] I had seen it before, but thought to view it again. At the time the film was made, Ava was about thirty-five years old, and with the camera again supplying a soft focus she looked none the worse for wear. But the story itself turns out to be totally confused. Apparently, there wasn't enough material in Ernest Hemingway's book, so parts from his later book, *A Farewell to Arms*, were also included.[5] The Polish nurse he was in love with in the earlier book was collapsed into Lady Brett Ashley in the later one. This dual character was played by Ava Gardner.

> *Though she loves Jake, she is unwilling to commit to a relationship with him because it will mean giving up sex. Indeed, she is unwilling to commit fully to any of the many men who become infatuated with her, though she has affairs with a number of them. However, she does not seem to draw much happiness from her independence. Her life, like the lives of many in her generation, is aimless and unfulfilling.*

Then instead of marital ties of each, Hemmingway and his love interest were both married, which is the "reality" from which the book was taken, preventing a sexual union. Hemingway, to somewhat disguise the fictious relationship makes himself impotent from war injuries. Lady Ashley, in the book and film, has many relationships, attempting to satisfy her yearning for Jack Barnes. But she will not be satisfied by substitutes. This, we eventually learn, prevents consummation of their mutual attraction. In other words, instead of depicting Lady Ashley as encumbered by a loveless marriage, Hemmingway decides to make her male love interest impotent.

Does this transposition work? Not at all. Why? Because sexually, men are not that different from one another. If she could be satisfied, one man would probably be nearly as good as another. At least, even attributing something to technique, it would not make her dysfunctional, and it would not require very many men to find a winner. Actuality, it's because she cannot be satisfied by anyone—she tries one man after the other. Naturally, they all flunk the test. In other words, the problem is her, not him.

Of course, Hemingway's failure to deal properly with women is generic. His many marriages, and the women he picked to marry, testify to the fact that he had no real idea of women at all. In his stories they are all consigned to the bleachers, where their role is to root for our hero. Any doubt on the point is satisfied if we recall the sex scene with the peasant girl—who had been raped—in *For Whom the Bell Tolls* from 1940.[6]

> *On the way back to Pablo's camp, Robert Jordan and Maria make love in the forest. When they catch up with Pilar, Maria confesses to Pilar that the earth moved as they made love. Pilar, impressed, says that such a thing happens no more than three times in a person's lifetime.*

After they have sex, Robert Jordan, the male character, asks her...

> *For him it was a dark passage which led to nowhere, then to nowhere, then again to nowhere, once again to nowhere, always and forever to nowhere, heavy on the elbows in the earth to nowhere, dark, never any end to nowhere, hung on all time always to unknowing nowhere, this time and again for always to nowhere, now not to be borne once again always and to nowhere, now beyond all bearing up, up, up and into nowhere, suddenly, scaldingly, holdingly all nowhere gone and time absolutely still and they were both there, time having stopped and he felt the earth move out and away from under them." After a little while, he asks, "But did thee feel the earth move?" and she says yes, "And then the earth moved. The earth never moved before?" He assures her it truly never before had for him.*

But really the question and answer clangs like a cowbell. It's like J. P. Morgan sailing down the Hudson River, with a boat full of guests, when a man asks how much a boat like this costs. JP says if you have to ask you can't afford it. The answer to the Q&A here is the same: If you have to ask, it didn't happen. And not only did it not happen, but even asking the question reveals an unlikely "everyman for himself" approach to sex, not likely to produce disclosures.

As a matter of fact, Hemingway is not alone in wearing masculine blinders. Selecting Ava Gardner for the role is an indication of a dysfunctional Hollywood-producer, male-view of the whole thing. She was married three times, to Mickey Rooney, Artie Show, and Frank Sinatra for one year, two years, and three years, respectively. Even if Mickey Rooney was not the most stable candidate, Frank Sinatra left his wife for her, so he was very serious.

Testimony from Ava Gardner herself is a clincher. In her memoirs she said sex was fine with Sinatra until she was on the way to the bidet. Evidently that's when things fell apart. A little witticism, to be sure, but beneath the humor lay a truth, and it is a capstone on the question of orgasm. For if she was in a bad mood then, and typically so from her statement, immediately after sex, then she experienced no emotional release from the act. If that typified the situation, it means she really wasn't participating.

Standing at the end of the line of Ava's unsuccessful marriages was Frank Sinatra. The assumption must be that if he knew that there were three kinds of women, and that Ava was the inorgasmic variety, he would have acted differently. He would not have been so jealous. He would not have been afraid to leave her alone. He would not have flown to Africa to make sure that Clark Gable, or someone else was not in her tent at night or anytime. Why bother? In other words, this information might have changed his entire life. He might not have married her. He might not have left his wife. He might have held his family together. So it was very important for him, not to be wrong in his estimate of this woman. Nonetheless, he was totally misguided in his expectations.

To say that Hollywood producers are not too smart either, makes some sense. Obviously they don't care how good or bad an actress's sex life actually is. It's what they project on the screen that is of importance. Producers were interested in the screen "image" of the star. And the "image" turns out to be quite fragile, quite unreliable when you are dealing with a frigid woman or inorgasmic woman.

Ava's sexual unresponsiveness is not unique in Hollywood. Two other screen "love goddesses," Rita Hayworth and Marilyn Monroe, are virtual carbon copies, at least comparing the emotion of their screen images with the lack of response in real life. Rita (1918–87) came before Ava (1922–90), and Marilyn (1926–62). In all three there was a radical disconnect between screen image and street reality. Even standing alone they almost prove Fanny Brice's question and answer. Her rhetorical question: "Why do so many rich and famous men go for frigid women?" Her answer: "Because they are such good actresses." Good actresses, at least, in this special sense of good enough to fool the men in their lives. To be sure *Redbook* magazine reports that 52 percent of women regularly fake an orgasm. So they are not in any sense in unique or select company. But they are unique in the heights of professionalism they achieved by being sexy, contrasted with their apparent inability to play any kind of sexual role in reality.[7]

To be sure, the three were not the same psychological types. Employing psychoanalyst Carl Jung's philosophical types—Ava was an extrovert, Rita Hayworth was an introvert, and Marilyn Monroe was an ambivert. But Marilyn not found in a Jungian middle where extremes are reconciled as one reaches maturity. This is the middle where both types are present, but not reconciled.

Our "love goddesses" are different not only in this respect, but in the kind of family discord and neglect, they endured as children. Marilyn's was so bad; one wonders how she could have survived at all. Nonetheless, all were scared by neglect or inattention.

Rita, for example, did not like to be the center of things, but after a photo spread as centerfold of *Life Magazine* on a bed in a negligee, the photo became the number one pinup of World War II and she became Hollywood's number one love goddess. This position was confirmed by her appearance in the film "Gilda" where she sang "Put the Blame on Mame," while slowly peeling off elbow-length gloves in lieu of her evening dress.

But look at her history. She was performing from an early age with her father as her constant companion. There's supposition that he molested her and she married her first husband to get away from her father. Her first husband, Edward Judson, managed her affairs from 1937 to 1942, when she divorced him to marry Victor Mature, but surprising everyone when she married Orson Welles instead.

The marriage didn't last. Next she met Aly Khan on a trip to Europe. He was still married, so their affair received indignant and widespread criticism. Somewhat in reaction he divorced his wife and married Rita in 1949. They divorced two years later. Dick Haymes was next, but here again it lasted only two years. Finally, there was director James Hill with a marriage of three years.

What happened? What were all these marriages about? No one asks much less suggests any explanation. As Stanley Frank has stated, quoting Dr. Wilhelm Stekel, "The frigid woman receives only slight attention in literature, public opinion even elevates her infirmity to the rank of a virtue and gives it a heroic varnish, whereas the virtuous man succumbs to the curse of ridicule."[8] This is surely true in Hollywood.

In short, the explanation is obvious. Two divorces usually tell the tale. Sex without orgasm is intolerable. With Rita there are five marriages all with an average span of two years. From a male point of view, the question repeats itself. If Orson Welles had known from the outset that he was dealing with an inorgasmic woman would he have married her? Or Aly Khan? Would he have divorced his wife if he knew?

Marilyn Monroe completes our story of the difference between screen image and the uninspired reality of Hollywood's "love goddesses." She was illegitimate. Her mother was a negative cutter at Columbia and RKO Studios, before her confinement in a mental institution. Marilyn was shuttled from foster home to an orphanage to a friend of her mother's and incidentally or not so incidentally she was a victim of a rape—before her first marriage.

At sixteen she quit high school and married Jim Dougherty with whom she said it was less than a loveless marriage, it was a silent one too. With World War II he was shipped overseas. She posed for a nude calendar photo, and its almost universal reproduction in serviceman's lockers launched her career.

Divorced from Dougherty she married Joe DiMaggio, but that lasted only nine months. Next was Arthur Miller who divorced his wife to marry her. She adopted Judaism for him. An affair with Elia Kazan, among others, and four years later, she divorced Miller. She had an affair with President John F. Kennedy then was passed around to others, possibly his brother, Robert Kennedy. She became depressed, threatened to call the media and was found overdosed in her apartment.

Passing more involved plots concerning possible fowl play in her death—irrelevant to our inquiry—we find Lee Strasberg of the New School eulogizing her saying, "Marilyn Monroe was a legend. In her own lifetime she created a myth of what a poor girl from a deprived background could attain. For the entire world she became the symbol of the eternal feminine."

If that was indeed her role, symbols have nothing to do with realities. Arthur Miller reported that those two years in his life was time swept down the drain by her crazy behavior and ceaseless demands. The point to be made is that he obviously did not know what he was dealing with or the virtual nonexistence of any possibility of a happy life with America's symbol of the "eternal feminine."

We don't have to speculate. She has stated quite frankly, "I have never had an orgasm." In short with all three "love goddesses" it is clear that the on-screen sexuality bared little resemblance to the off-screen reality. Rita Hayworth, Ava Gardner, and Marilyn Monroe provide three powerful examples. The absolute *ne plus ultra* of feminine sexuality on screen complete failures in their sex lives off-screen. This is like the images in Plato's cave, where the shadows on the wall bear little resemblance to the three-dimensional reality of their actual lives. For our purposes, men seriously searching for women, it appears obvious that if the men in the lives of these women knew that there were three subspecies they were involved with these disastrous choices might have been avoided.

Orson Welles seems to have his main interest elsewhere. He states that during the war a man had more sex than he could possibly handle. So he did not fret particularly the loss of Rita. But Arthur Miller, by his own admission, was completely out of his depth with Marilyn. And Frank Sinatra was beside himself attempting to control an uncontrollable situation with Ava. They were all looking for some kind of stability, but they were looking for it where there was no possibility of finding it.

CHAPTER 3
On the Way to the Bidet

One searches in vain in modern psychoanalysis and mainstream media for a full recognition of the justice of the ancient Medea's lament: "If your life at night is good, you think you have everything: but if in that quarter things go wrong, you will consider your best and truest interests most hateful" (Euripides, _Medea_ [431 BC], trans. Rex Warner).[1]

Or consider the statement made a millennium later and a continent distant, by Persian poet and prose writer Sa'di, who observed that: "Much contention and strife will arise in that house where the wife shall get up dissatisfied with her husband" (Gulistan [AD 1258]).[2]

To the same effect, but not to arouse the ire of Christian censors, is Ogden Nash's humorous ditty: "When a lady's erotic life is vexed, God knows what God is coming next."[3]

The problem for a man looking for the right woman—the topic of this inquiry—is that while women rap about men, men rarely rap about women (at least in the same vein). Here, for example, is an article by Maureen Dowd, in the _New York Times_, from July 6, 2008, entitled "An Ideal Husband," or, how to avoid ending up like Christie Brinkley or Madonna.[4]

Actually, Ms. Dowd is not giving the advice, merely sponsoring it. The advice is given by a seventy-nine-year-old Catholic priest who has spent his celibate life allegedly "mulling connubial bliss." I say allegedly because for forty years he actually has been giving advice, not on that topic, but on the opposite one of "Whom not to marry." In other words, he is working the same side of the street as the topic of this essay.

Father Pat Connor is his name. He sums up his advice by stating a woman should "Never marry a man who has no friends, or a man who is financially irresponsible, or one who is too agreeable in word and deed, or a man who is too attached to his mother's apron strings, or to a man with no sense of humor, or the strong silent type, or one with a problem of drink or drugs, or one who hails from a family with a history of divorce, or whose deepest beliefs, notably religious, are radically different from your own, or, finally, he should be a good person which is demonstrated by having the human skills to be willing to forgive, to give praise and be courteous."

At this point Maureen's cronies allegedly cry: "But you've eliminated everyone!" To my mind, it would actually be a strange cry, given that all these conditions might be met, and you would still have nothing but an empty suit, which is possibly what Ms. Dowd has in mind. As far as the idea of financial responsibility is concerned this is advice that men need more than women since women are by far the most financial irresponsible, according to my experience in bankruptcy cases. Granted gambling sometimes gets away from men, but it gets away from women as well.

As far as excessive attachment to mom is concerned, this is another bit of advice, which is more for men than for women, the recipients of Father Connor's quoted advice. Since men may like to have their moms around to do things for them (another angle)—is a plus for women, it is women and not men who imitate their mothers. In fact these imitations of mother by daughter are things men should be particularly keen to take note of because if you don't like the mom, it's pretty certain you will not like her daughter after the first attraction wears off.

Drink and drugs cuts both ways, but again the advice is more for men than for women, since women have an almost impossible time reforming a bad habit. They say: "Well, this one time will not hurt. I will quit tomorrow." But tomorrow never comes, and this habit takes them down the tubes.

Similarly, a divorce in the family is a much greater danger signal in a woman than in a man precisely because women absorb their mother's values, while men not at all or less so. In fact, it is my experience when working in a hospital some years ago that women frequently decide to marry with this reservation secretly in mind that if it doesn't work, you can always get a divorce. I was naively shocked when I first heard this coming from a student nurse.

As far as what makes a good person (I thought that's what all these items were about?), forgiveness, giving praise, and being courteous— these may be what receives Ms. Dowd's vote, but they sound abysmally empty to me. They are strictly *How to Win Friends and Influence People.*[5] "Can I interest you in this model Chevrolet?"

To see this advice in its most chiaroscuro dimension, we should go back and compare it to a pagan's predecessor (a convenient Christian, if erroneous reference.) Aristotle for example considers the same question in his *Nicomachaen Ethics*, and comes up with some rather different elements. With respect to his primary virtues first comes not forgiveness, but courage on which he spends many pages detailing its kinds and characteristics. Then is temperance, especially with money and pleasures of the body, then pride, next ambition, good temper, friendliness, truthfulness and ready wit and last justice. Twelve in all.[6]

All these virtues are found in the middle ground between too much and too little as for example with courage where too little is described as cowardice and too much as foolhardiness.

Now the startling thing in this comparison is this. Next to Aristotle's list the list in Ms. Dowd's article sounds more like the qualifications for a valet than for a groom. The reason is Christian virtues are mostly negative in the sense that the Ten Commandments, for example, are a list of don'ts. Only two do not prohibit something, Keep holy the Sabbath, and Honor your father and your mother. The rest are prohibitory: Don't worship strange gods, Don't take the Lord's name in vain, Don't kill anyone, Don't commit adultery, Don't steal, Don't bear false witness, and Don't covet your neighbor's wife or goods.

In comparison with Maureen's list, the so-called pagan virtues of Aristotle are not negative, like Father Connor's, but positive. They concern things that one should do. Courage, for example, is concerned with doing something and doing it right. In Father Connor's list, on the other hand, to forgive, to give praise, and be courteous, are negative in the sense that one does not have to get up from one's easy chair to perform them.

In this respect, made much of by Frederick Nietzsche (1844–1900), Pagan and Christian ethics take radically different paths to find the good life. Christian ethics is concerned with what one should not do which Pagan ethics with what one should do. The first is negative; the second is positive. And it is here, perhaps, that we see Nietzsche's point: that the transforming character of Christianity is such that it leaves a person undefined virtually invisible. And this in turn because no list of negative rules, however long, adds up to anything positive to a positive person. If the purpose of life is action, negative characteristics provide no guide whatsoever.

So in the case of Christianity we have prohibitory rules, and in the case of Pagan reasoning the best way to act. The one leads to the holy life with the possibility of happiness in the afterlife while the second to the possibility of happiness in the here and now.

There are a couple of other things in this Christian/Pagan comparison to notice, however, one in agreement, the other disagreement with our essay. In a romantic scenario we agree with Father Connor in counseling attention to important questions before falling too seriously in love, because "infatuation trumps judgment," and advice is too late afterward. No doubt about it.

Where we depart most strongly from the positive/negative aspect of his advice is on the question of sex. Father Pat Connor seems not concerned at all with the subject matter of our inquiry, namely sexual relations. And this, of course, is based on the concern that sexual relations, to a Catholic, are for the purpose of having children, not for the purpose of personal gratification.

Whereas our position in this essay is that sexual gratification is one of the main concerns in a male/female relationship. And apart from Ms. Dowd's sponsorship of the contrary view, women do discuss these topics, but men generally do not. As a result, men enter relationships in nearly total ignorance of a woman's sexuality learning years later what they should have known before the relationship or marriage. Like anyone of our random collection of rich and famous men, and a woman, who were apparently oblivious to what their sex partner was experiencing, or not experiencing in the relationship. Hence, it is to fill the void that is conversationally absent, that this essay is written.

But it is not merely to fill the existent void that the Christian/Pagan antithesis is treated. It is with us still though somewhat disguised. Thus in a book written by Marilyn Yalom entitled, "How the French Invented Love," from the *The Wall Street Journal* in 2012, she compares French with American attitudes toward love and sex. She advises that while 83 percent of American thought that true love can exist without a radiant sex life, only 34 percent of the French believed it. A 50 percent difference! What accounts for this vast difference?[7]

Obviously Maureen Dowd's or Father Connor's Christian views on pre-marriage play a role in producing this vast difference. But what role? That is the question. With 83 percent saying sex is not an essential element, even those in divorce court with sexual maladjustment as their chief complaint must so hold being among the 83 percent. In other words their beliefs and their conduct appear to be on two completely different tracks. The point, however, is that the beliefs of this 83 percent are in the Christian mold while their conduct is otherwise. With the French, on the other hand, this 34 percent who said "true love could exist without a radiant sex life" is exactly the one-third who never experienced orgasm in the American poll. The inference therefore is that Americans bow to mainstream opinion while the French do not.

The reason behind these conflicting opinions, Ms. Yalom concludes is because in France, sex desire is not optional. "A Frenchman or woman without sex desire is considered defective, like someone missing a sense of taste or smell." In America with the Christian lobby it is almost the opposite.

CHAPTER 4
"Fake It Until You Can Make It"

The ten indications or symptoms of inorgasmic women to be considered in the next chapter have one feature in common. They all, more or less, rely on the advice that has been laid at Hillary Clinton's doorstep, by columnist Maureen Dowd, the *New York Times* (June 8, 2012) "Fake it until you can make it."[1] The question that arises from the advice to fake it, belongs to Fanny Brice from the Ziegfield Follies, who was asked: "How do they get away with it?" Her answer, in so many words: "Because they are such good actresses." Of course, this may get the women who employ this devise to the altar, but what happens beyond the ceremony is another question.

Then too, some contributory male blindness is also required. Take the case of Hillary Clinton, who herself is charged with offering this advice. How did it work for her? To ask this question is virtually to answer it, it didn't work. Bill Clinton's continuous philandering was a cause of constant hostilities in their marriage.

Actually faking it really doesn't work long term for anyone. The simple reason is that "arguments start on the way to the bidet," to quote Ava Gardner. In other words it requires more than the heavy breathing and loud sighs of Meg Ryan in the film *When Harry Met Sally*, to convince anyone who is really interested in what is taking place in the female psyche. There is the aftermath, or Post Coitum, when faking it breaks down. The good mood is gone, and the wicked witch replaces the good fairy.

If the woman was not participating, she grows increasingly displeased at always playing the applauding audience to your Academy Award sexual performance, displeasure grows to annoyance, and annoyance to outright hatred, and that's the effective end of an intimacy in the relationship or marriage.

In Hillary's case, all one needs to do is to look at her in the media. She has increasingly taken on the male persona. But Hillary is a single case. The question is how do the 52 percent—accordingly to a *Redbook* survey—who fake it, make it? The answer appears to be that they make it, in the sense of getting by, only if their male relationship is too indifferent of care or notice.[2]

Of course, Ernest Hemingway's example supplies potential testimony that many men, intelligent men in other areas, can go through life without ever finding out what their partner is feeling or thinking. They feel the pain, but they never discover what is causing it.

But how and why does a woman get herself into a marital situation, when she is not equipped to carry through with it? One answer, regularly supplied, it that neither her thinking nor planning extend beyond the ceremony. She is thinking of what she will be getting out of the marriage, not what she must be putting in to it.

Actually, when a man and a woman meet in a romantic liaison, they have a number of discordant goals they are attempting to satisfy. And goals, not obligations, tend to be uppermost in their minds. Goals of men and women are frequently quite different, and not, as in traditional agricultural societies, in harmony or interrelated. What the man ordinarily wants and needs is sexual satisfaction and a working or intellectual partner.

What the woman wants breaks down into three possibilities—according to the taxonomy with which we began this book. For the sexually orgasmic woman, she may participate in sex to her and her partner's mutual satisfaction, but she is not excessively interested in his work. To the frigid woman, in default of sexual satisfaction, she is quite interested in his work, but has little or no interest in sex. As my bartender friend tells it, "my first wife was well informed, but she had little interest in sex; my second wife is great in bed, but she has little interest in politics or current affairs. I guess you get one or the other," he advises. Actress Ingrid Bergman agrees with the proposition. She relates that she was too interested in intellectual matters to have much passion left for sex.

The typical man, on the other hand, is not a totally innocent bystander. For he wants to convince the woman involved that he is sensitive, patient, and understanding—*more* sensitive, patient and understanding it unfortunately turns out than he actually is. In short, both the man and the woman in the play-acting are too concerned with the plausibility of his or her own performance to notice the discrepancies in their companion.

Thus, in spite of their possible attempt to be forthcoming, both are trying to convince the other of something that is not quite true. After the ceremony, they gradually wake up to the fact that they are not going to get exactly what they bargained for. In the case of a woman who has never had an orgasm, this period of adjustment is murderous. You can only fake it for so long, and then the fact becomes you simply do not care that much.

Jumping ahead and considering the symptoms to be surveyed, we find that most divorces occur in the fourth and fifth years of marriage. One theory is that serotonin levels tend to drop about that time and sexual attraction drops with it. And if sexual attractiveness ends, what's left?

Another related theory is that testosterone and serotonin are contrary indicators. When serotonin is down, testosterone is up. And while testosterone governs sexual attraction, serotonin governs love or friendship. Hence a fall in serotonin levels gives testosterone a chance to operate, according to one medical theory.

A statistic published some years ago found that a high percentage of women are no happier in their second marriages than in their first. The inference being, the problem is not Tom, Dick, or Harry, it doesn't matter who it is; it's any regular relation with any man that's the problem. Of course, it is quite possible that if a female mate keeps picking her dad for a husband, and if she has had a bad relationship with her father, this will be repeated with any selection of husbands.

Often women learn this unhappy fact after two or three tries. The question is why you—the man in the picture—should suffer the consequences of a situation settled before you entered the scene.

In her biography, Barbara Walters owns that she was not meant for marriage. But one wonders whether she revealed that fact to her third husband. Or was it after a period of mutual suffering that she decided to come clean? The point is that women have some responsibility for knowing themselves, and for telling prospective grooms about their antipathies. An enormous amount of suffering might be avoided if they did.[3]

And there is this to consider. If the divorce rate is approximately 50 percent in the United States, and the rate of women who fake it is 52 percent according to *Redbook*, then there is at least a good chance these two percentages are related and an important question to ask what percentage of the latter folds into the former? In other words, how many women who fake it, soon get tired and seek a divorce? Over 50 percent of divorces occur in the first ten years of marriage; over 30 percent in the first four years.

In America, at least, these considerations lead to the necessity for a proposal, that some premarital counseling may be in order, to warn the most vulnerable persons that such a marriage may not last, for reasons on earth in the here and now, and not for reasons in an afterlife in heaven, attended to by Father Connor—treated in the last chapter.

In summary then, faking it doesn't work. Girls who learned to say no in their earliest years and have been saying it until their late teens and early twenties—or later—are not suddenly going to say yes when the situation signals the need to do so. Rather arguments will start on the way to the bidet.

And arguments on the way to the bidet will soon spread to cover the entire relationship. But this is a book primarily for men and how to avoid these very real hazards. Thus the next chapter deals with the particularities of these crucial questions.

CHAPTER 5
Ten Leading/Misleading Symptoms

Introduction

n this chapter we review ten leading symptoms of an inorgasmic disorder. As you review these you will see that they have been developed as a method of avoiding revelation of the fact that the woman counter posing such symptoms is inorgasmic. The crux of the problem is complicated by the fact that not all inorgasmic women know, or are continuously conscious that they can not have an orgasm, and they often wander into a seductive scenario without full awareness of their own disability.

Thus to begin this chapter with (i) 'Two Strikes,' men frequently become involved with a woman who is twice divorced. We have stated that such a woman is highly unlikely to be orgasmic. Doesn't the woman know it? Sometimes yes, sometimes no, and sometimes some middle ground of half-consciousness that occupies the space between knowing and not knowing. Sometimes a woman wants companionship. Sometimes she wants a husband. So in order to have a husband she must delude herself into thinking that she can sustain a relationship that didn't work the first time. Unless she gets married for the third time, only to find the same disability that has ended marriages in the past has ended this fresh at-tempt now. And so another misadventure.

In sub-chapter (ii), an inorgasmic woman, not knowing her disabil-ity which has been buried beneath an array of distractions which have been interposed for the very purpose of preventing recognition of her situation.

In sub-chapter (iii) 'Control Freak,' the same mechanism is used but magnified, to the point of near hysteria. In sub-chapter (iv), we have a woman who recognizes her symptoms, but blames the ineptitude of men she has met for her disability. This time, she will 'fake it until she can make it,' but at long last it becomes obvious that this solution will not work.

In sub-chapter (v), 'Hyper-indecision,' her disability presents itself as an inability to make a decision and stick to it. Intentions are revised and then re-revised without providing a solution. Sub-chapter (vi) 'Nothing in Moderation,' —is a variation of the inability to make a decision and stick to it. Here that failure is recognized and to meet it she interposes an exaggerated response to a situation.

Sub-chapter (vii), 'Let's Be Friends,' is another situation where the mechanism for solution is to avoid sexual situations altogether.

Sub-chapter (viii), 'Delinquent Dads,' are doubtless the being the cause or the half-cause of the woman's disability. Dad prescribed too much or not enough, or the wrong kind of instruction, advice and discipline.

Sub-chapter (ix), 'Mindful Moms,' brings on the other half of 'Delinquent Dads,' by supplying constant criticism of the father's in-ept behavior.

Finally, sub-chapter (x), 'Post Coitum,' offers the final clue, by pass-ing off the sexual experience as 'O.K.,' and adding that fighting only be-gins "On the way to the bidet."

In summary, these symptoms, if seen for what they are, will caution a man to avoid disastrous entanglement with those afflicted.

(i) Two Strikes

If the woman who attracts you is once divorced, you are wading in deep waters; twice divorced is suicidal for a man seeking sexual satisfaction in his relations with a woman. When you look at divorce statistics and find that nearly 50 percent of marriages end in divorce, you should tack our *New York Times* taxonomy on the wall next to it and ask yourself, which of the three subgroups make up most of these divorces. Just to pose the question automatically puts you on the right track. The group most heavily represented is the inorgasmic group. And they are closely followed by the "sometimes, but as little as possible" group.

By the time of the second divorce, sex patterns and problems have become hard core behavior. Continuously having sex when you don't have desire becomes the next thing to being regularly raped. Some theories make it universal: all sex is rape. It's when you don't want to that makes it seem that way. And for inorgasmic women seldom in the mood, soon becomes never. Her reaction is that sexual antipathy hardens into seething hatred.

Why I didn't see this earlier in my legal career is a puzzle. As a divorce lawyer I do several divorce interviews a week. And in this position the sex problem is right there on the interview questionnaire. But I suppose that looking at each divorce as an individual phenomenon, one is less likely to be aware of generalizations that may be made. Then too, people getting a divorce do not clearly see the basic problem. They are commonly deflected by the immediate situation. What she is complaining about—be it money, division of chores, your inattention, sloppy habits, and the like— these are distractions from the real problem buried beneath an array of pseudo-problems put in their place.

In other words, the micro-problems captured our attention and we did not have enough interest left over for the macro-problems behind them. I did not see the real issue for the same reason that divorce clients did not see the real issue—they were too deflected by the pseudo-problems or micro-problems put in their place, and they didn't feel like talking about it anyway.

Of course, if divorces among first married is already heavily weighted toward sexual dysfunction, by the time you get to a second divorce, sexual dysfunction is numero uno. In the Navy, it's called "General Quarters!" Run, don't walk to the nearest exit! Whatever you do, don't believe her: it was not her husband's fault. Once perhaps, twice no. She couldn't reveal her sex problem, even to herself.

If you have any lingering doubts, have a look at some of the celebrity divorces in the news. Here we get some reportage of the underside of marriage—otherwise lacking. Look at divorces involving such notables as, for example, Marilyn Monroe, Barbara Stanwick, Lana Turner, Rita Hayworth, Ava Gardner, Martha Gelhorn, Kristy Brinkley—all of whom had several husbands and eventually admit to antipathy to sex.

But don't be shy. If you feel uncertain, do what a friend of mine used to do. Look up one of her ex-husbands or boyfriends, invite them out for a drink, and listen patiently to his side of the story. In my experience men are fairer, more reliable witnesses than women, who hate to be blamed for a failed marriage—despite (or because of) the fact that marriage was her idea in the first place.

You might ask yourself, why a woman twice divorced would want to get married again? Of course, money is the first answer, at least if the *Financial Times* is accurate, when they report that 60 percent of females would marry mainly for money. And if the woman is over thirty years of age, the number goes up to 70 percent.[1]

The next reason for a failed marriage is when what she really wants is companionship. Look at the "Women Seeking Men" column in any newspaper or journal: "loves music, dancing, motorcycles, outdoors, movies, and creative pursuits." This is a real ad! The longer the list of diversions, the less time there is for sex. If you allot one day for music, one day for dancing, and so forth, it leaves one day for sex—if you never have to work late. In any case, the longer the list, the less likely that sex is going to figure anywhere on it.

The fact is, the less interested she is in sex the less likely she is to read anything about it. Not being too interested or well-educated in the sexual end of marriage, really not wanting to know anything about it, she supposes that all women have similar disinclinations. She does not know where she stands in the *New York Times* taxonomy, or even that it exists. Hence, she supposes that all women must negotiate a husband's sexual demands down to the minimum.[2]

In the Victorian era, it was supposed that women in general did not care for sex. A likely duty that just had to be performed was the suggestion. Thus the British witticism, "I just look at the wall and think of the Queen." It was not that no one cared for it, but no one talked about it. Or if they did, they talked about it with disdain, or as a method of having children, or on the other side of it, engaging in birth control. Like Sigmund Freud's wife, who simply announced she intended henceforth to be celibate. A judgment from which there was no appeal.

That's at least the picture from a rational viewpoint. From an irrational one, there are as many split views as there are split minds. I mean women who exhibit one personality in public, another in private.

Frequently, inorgasmic women start a sexual relationship with enthusiasm, a natural enthusiasm born of a belief that with a new love affair comes the possibility of a new attitude, and with a new attitude, new possibilities. Unfortunately, it takes two people to make a love affair. One new love is only half of the equation. As a friend said to me in Paris, "A lot of people come here to get away from it all. The problem is they bring themselves with them." It took twenty, thirty, or forty years to form that personality; a comparable amount of time must be taken to un-form or reform it—and a will to do it, which is the thing most often lacking.

In any case, this new love enthusiasm quickly fades, and before long they are thinking, if not saying, what one woman in a moment of irrepressible candor blurted out: "I divorced my husband because I didn't want to fuck him. Why should I fuck you?" I had to suppress a laugh because this affair was several months old at the time, and this remark belongs at the beginning of a relationship and not at the end. And then at the bluntness of her remark. In any case, my response was: "I can't think of any reason—except it was your idea in the first place," but she wasn't listening.

Strangely, the gist of this exchange is not unique. Inorgasmic women often regard the last time as the first time. If you were in the bedroom last time, they do not want to go to the bedroom. Because I suppose, the place reminds them of their failure to have an orgasm in that place. Similarly they do not wish to hear any reference to what occurred the last time you had relations. You are always starting, in effect, with a clean slate.

(ii) Self-Hypnosis

You can see the obsessive-compulsive type, so you don't have to get too close to identify her. Is she an exercise-a-holic, school-a-holic, or ad-dicted to some other compulsive repetitive behavior? And what's the connection between such behavior and being inorgasmic? The answer to the last question is that she has an almost impossible time attempting to get off her conveyor belt long enough to make an emotional commit-ment to anything or anyone other than her "idea fixe."

As with most human behavior however, cause and effect are con-fused with loopback or feedback. Thus the workaholic's love life may suffer from compulsive behavior, about which she complains, but it is probably to avoid emotional commitments that her life is organized around such mechanical or obsessive commitments in the first place.

Since most romances start in the workplace, compulsive behavior is not hard to see. She gets to work early. Possibly she leaves work late as well. Her commitment to work seems out of proportion to the work being done. Most women who work in offices soon find that a man's commitment to the job is unappealing. There are other things in life, you will hear them say. Actually, the other things are not particularly appealing to men.

Barbara Walters's biography, *Audition*, presents a showcase illustra-tion of a workaholic. For a long time I was casually on the lookout for facts about Ms. Walters with which to confirm my intuitions about her. It has all the facts you require to understand her sex life, or lack of it. All you need is the courage to attack the five-hundred plus pages of chit-chat in which this information is buried.[1]

She had a cold or somewhat detached father, who did not encourage physical familiarity (p. 16). Her mother, on the other hand, was mostly a homemaker who did not have a lot to say. But at least her mother was affectionate. "To be with my mother was my greatest pleasure," Walters relates. What conversation she had with her mother took the form of complaints about her father. She was "the recipient of most of her [mother's] lamentations, usually about my father." These were about "their lack of money, and about his absence when she needed him" (p. 18).

Married three times to Bob Katz, Lee Guber, and Merv Adelson as well as an extended relationship with Alan Greenspan (then CEO of Bear Sterns), she knew her first marriage was a mistake going into it. As a matter of fact, she felt the same way all three times. "My heart never felt so heavy, but then again, my heart would feel just as heavy every time I married (I've been married three times) which is why, as I write this, please know I will never marry again."

It was not that her first husband was physically unattractive, but she "felt little sexual desire for him." (p. 83) In fact, "that dull bedspread seemed like a perfect symbol of the marriage." (p. 16) Actually, after her second divorce, she had already decided, "I was no good at marriage and that basically the failure was my fault." (p. 214) Nonetheless, for some unaccountable reason she married a third time, with the same result.

Summing up her life, Walters was asked by Oprah: "What does being Barbara Walters mean?" Her answer is revealing. "I'm not sure. I realize how blessed I have been but sometimes I still feel inadequate. I don't cook. I can't drive. Most of the time when I look back on what I've done, I think—Did I do that? Why didn't I enjoy it more? Was I working too hard to see?" And she added: "Most hard working women would understand what we felt." (*Oprah Winfrey Show*, September 17, 2004)

In other words, a kind of emptiness. She met many of the most important influential people in the world, but looking back on it, she simply feels an emptiness. She felt empty because holding up a microphone and asking celebrities questions is an empty task. It's the workaholic syndrome.

In any case, away from the job, we find a school-a-holic or an exercise-a-holic. The school-a-holic is always involved in a school project. Nothing diverts her mind from that problem or what the professor considers important. She is hyper-alert about it and its implications. Dead to other topics she is working for approval, and the professor is not going to applaud anything less. She is going to be best in the class. Only superiority will be noticed. If she is second or third, she is already suffering.

They say that grades are not very good indicators of success in life. And the same authorities wonder why. The reason is that grades are given on the basis of memorization of verbal materials; and memorization of verbal materials is not the key to success in anything. A previous Secretary of State, Condoleezza Rice, is probably our best example of why memorization of verbal materials rarely leads to anything more. Her skill is one of saying the right thing at the right time. This rarely has anything to do with success at any task that involves putting a skill to imaginative use.

The girl who lives for the gym may be similarly described. She has the newest, most chic exercise outfit. She doesn't work out for one hour but two. She speaks with real interest about calisthenics or weight lifting, whatever it is. And she hates to leave the place. Watch them workout, or linger after a workout, and you ask yourself: what's the point? What are they trying to prove? It's really not fitness, which might be accomplished in half the time. The answer finally becomes plain—it's called an obsession. A train comes by going in this direction; they got on. And here they are. That's all there is to it.

In yoga, they are the ones who develop the backache. Jogging, it is their knees that give way. In karate, they again hurt their knees or legs. Women's knees are not as strong as men's; hence, they should take special note of the fact that they are not men and their bodies have different needs. But given the existing notion that men and women are the same, they are not keen to learn of essential and disqualifying differences, which accordingly tend to be their special weak points.

The workaholic, the school-a-holic and the exercise-a-holic are merely three examples of obsessive-compulsive behavior, which is what we are ultimately getting at. What is it about such behavior that can be identified with sexual dysfunction? That is what we wish to underline. And perhaps more importantly, does this behavior come first, sexual dysfunction second, or is it the reverse, or do they work synergistically? Doubtless the answer is all the above in the sense that, in some instances, it could be any of the three.

So what is the lesson of obsessive personalities? It's the difference between motivation and obsession. Being orgasmic does not mean not being motivated; it means not being obsessive.

There's a difference between motivation and obsession that we must make. We might diagram this by saying, motivation is from in front; obsession is from behind. The key is whether money is a tool, or a goal in itself. That's the determination a man must make. As a tool, you do not pursue a man for his money. The effort made must be in front. Take away the reward, and the effort ceases. With the obsessive-compulsive, on the other hand, take away the reward and the efforts continue with a new quickly substituted purpose. In short, in the one case, the reward explains the behavior, in the other—the obsessive-compulsive—the behavior is the goal that crowds out everything else.

(iii) Control Freak

Is she a control freak? Does she plan everything down to the last detail? Like the ex-wife of a friend of mine, vacation agendas were planned down to the date and time of every plane, train, bus, hotel, tour guide, and meal. Here she was in Detroit controlling every move of her husband and two daughters—vacationing in Europe—from across the ocean.

Of course, a personal confession—my travel schedules are exactly the opposite. Nothing is planned. Everything is freeform, so we spend a lot of time looking for the right hotel, as well as everything else. I am not contending that anyone should adopt my method (there is moderation); however, a schedule is fine, but you need a certain flexibility if you are to keep your brain working.

In any case, the holiday planner is one kind of control freak. Another is a woman who is so neat and clean, a spotless housekeeper, who has trees removed so she doesn't have to rake leaves in the fall. Does the automatic sprayer come on to water the lawn even when it is raining? Is she or her husband out there with a snow shovel when the first flakes hit the ground? Does she, in short, spin out of control (and characteristically develop a migraine) when things don't conform to her plans?

A third kind in the same genus might be a penny pincher. For it soon develops into a system whose justification is the system itself. One such was a friend of a friend, she called more than once and wanted to speak to me. We stopped at a coffee shop and she had an ice cream. What was it about? It's difficult to remember. What is not difficult to remember is that the conversation soon turned to the topic of sex.

She had been going (as I said) with a friend of mine, and they had broken up. His sexual demands were beyond her she said. He wanted sex all the time. In the morning, when she had to get to work, for example, they had a long verbal battle about the demands. I couldn't imagine the conversation. It would kill any interest I might have had on the subject.

She described their sex lives in detail; in such detail that I was somewhat embarrassed to listen. Actually in her mood of full disclosure, I should have asked more questions, but I didn't. I drove her home, and she, apparently stimulated by her own revelations, offered me a kiss, which turned into something more. But then she went in to her apartment, instructing me to call her.

The next time I went to her place, we sat on the couch and talked about a variety of subjects, somewhat indifferently. She evidently wanted me to make an advance, and I was cooperative. She was a bit tense. She announced that she felt somewhat uncomfortable. "You feel stiff, let me give you a message," she suggested. I thought that sounded like a good idea, and did as I was told taking off my shirt and loosening my pants belt. One thing led to another, and before you knew it, we were both in our skivvies. She was telling me something. I was investigating her anatomy. "Don't stop talking. Just let me move your—those—panties a little," I suggested. She went on talking, with an occasional breath catching start, while I ventured my hands into a new realm.

But the point to this story is to tag the extent of her control. I discovered this aspect of her personality as our relationship developed. In ensuing weeks and days, I learned that she prepared her lunches for the entire week on Sunday to save time, effort, and money. She counted every penny spent. She cut her hair short to save money. As a matter of fact, she gave me a lecture on better grooming. My hair should also be short, at least if I wanted to turn her on. And she wanted me to dress in a more conventional way, with the same end in mind.

Actually, penny pinching is just the most obvious feature of her life. It was a life that was almost mechanically ordered. From beginning to end she would harp on certain subjects, to the exclusion of everything else. She would look right through you when you were talking with a kind of commuter stare waiting impatiently for her turn.

Her favorite topic was the history (or myth) of feminine dominance. In prehistory, according to her tale, women dominated, and not only did they dominate, but they had multiple husbands, as you find in one of the three societies in Margaret Mead's *Coming of Age in Samoa*.

As far as I am concerned, I find myself more or less convinced by any argument on the subject of sexual roles, if it is reasonably presented. For the fact is no argument standing alone is going to change my behavior. I begin with a view that if you work for someone else forty hours a week you're a wage slave. The question then becomes one of whether the slaves are treated—and treat each other—more or less equitably. Is it fair? The answer in our society at a glance is that there are gross inequities throughout the system. The question of how it was or might have been at some remote pre-historical or mythological age does not have much bearing on that question.

Let's be fair. To survive everyone must exercise a certain amount of control over themselves in relation to their ability to control others. It's a balancing act. On the other hand, the control freak, properly so-called, is one who attempts to control the uncontrollable and is constantly freaked out when they cannot. Why are frigid women control freaks? The answer is because having an orgasm means losing control. Control is the key word in female orgasm. It means letting go. Control freaks cannot lose control even for an instant even for an orgasm.

In sex they contrive to be almost absolutely in control, as for example in our fourth case. "Kiss me," she virtually ordered on our second date. Then she offered me her open mouth. But where, I wondered, could we go from here—or there? I soon found out. Intercourse with her was actually outer course. It was like having sex with someone you never met. "When I got married," she confided, "I thought we could have sex around the clock." "Not if you go at it the way you do," I rejoined. "You must take it a little slower, if you wish it to last." In vain did I offer such helpful hints.

She had been married for twenty years, so this topic must have covered old ground. But she treated sex as if it were something new. Obviously, she could not have gone all night with anyone at that pace, or any other pace for that matter, so there must have been some interesting or uninteresting conversations with her ex. How could he, how did he, deal with this? Or was she more docile, less demanding during the marriage?

Unfortunately for my theories, my anthropological interest was insufficient to overcome my discomfort. I had to get away from this militant scenario. I felt like Giancarlo Giannini in the Italian film *Seven Beauties* (1976), held in a German prison and forced into a relationship with a fat guard as a means of escape.[1] To say my guard was good looking and that she had a fine figure seems superfluous. It didn't matter, I never felt quite so used as in this brief relationship.

What is the reason for such behavior? Obviously an inordinate desire for control is based on an earlier lack of control. And not only an earlier lack of control, but one which made the woman involved quite miserable. So now, she is imposing that same misery on the man in her life.

Hillary Clinton provides our last illustration. We all know or think we know something about her. Do you know that she's acted like a woman possessed from the earliest record of her actions? "Even in adolescence her self-confidence was evident," Carl Bernstein records in his 2007 biography, *A Woman in Charge*.[2]

In college she had already set her sights on a political position. She helped Bill Clinton in his second political campaign for governor acting at the time so driven that she alienated several of his regular workers.

Then in the White House, aides report that you did not say "Good Morning" to her, unless she first greeted you.

Her universal health care bill was defeated in a large part because of the total secrecy—basically the heavy-handed arrogance of the proceedings. Similarly, in losing her bid for presidency against Barack Obama, her campaign was obviously overdone, over-planned, over-scripted. It was all precast. Everyone was merely acting out their assigned role. The candidate was obviously gritting her teeth with determination through the primaries.

Hillary has always attempted to control the uncontrollable. As far as the desire is concerned, she had her mother's example. "As the chasm between Hillary and her father broadened during adolescence Hillary and her mother drew closer," relates Carl Bernstein (p. 27). But as far as her plan of action is concerned, that indomitable will to overcome obstacles, it was her father's refusal to give unqualified approval to her efforts, the refusal to acknowledge her success, which forms the basis for her firm determination. "As a child, Hillary tried every way she knew to please him and win his approval and they (the rest of the family) spent years seething at his treatment of her," Bernstein reports. (p. 16)

Bernstein is clear that it was her father's resistance that forms the basis for her ceaseless political efforts. But it was not only in politics. Aides described her as a "kind of classic bitchy wife…not quite putting her hand on her hip and finger wagging, but practically." (p. 27) As a matter of fact, her mother and father were "polar opposites—temperamentally, intellectually, and emotionally," according to Bernstein, "and their children could see that each grew increasingly exasperated with the other's evident ambivalence, antipathy and obvious resentment."

Thus Bill and Hillary's relationship was not merely a superficial repetition of her parent's relationship—it reflected it's deep structure. It was a matter of accepting, as a kind of norm, a repetition of that relationship.

Not merely the way things were; it was the way things should be. She became her mother. And Bill became (to Hillary) her father. It is this fact that makes her entire life seem robotic: the rules seemed to be in place before she was born. It only remained for her to appear to carry them out.

The word is "control." It is the very opposite of sexual satisfaction in a relationship. For as we have noted, a sexual orgasm abandons, or at least minimizes absolute control.

(iv) Pitch and Switch

Characteristically, when they are not in their celibate phase, frigid women come on very strong—enthusiastically. They will do anything for you. "I'm always available if you want to see me," insists Odette, in Proust's *Swann's Way*[1]—until she got him on the hook and role reversal kicked in. "We must get together and talk about your trip to Europe," I suggested to a flirtatious female, "but you're probably busy." To my surprise she responded: "I will make myself available whenever it suits you."

As Jackie Kennedy said (admitting more than she knew): "My greatest moral fault is that initial enthusiasms tend to fade very quickly, whether vertical or horizontal enthusiasms, former lovers doubtless would be inclined to add.

When the famous architect Frank Lloyd Wright's second wife was murdered, a divorcee from Texas wrote telling him how much she admired him. He was her hero, her ideal man, her dream man, and so forth. She visited him at Talesin, Wisconsin, and stayed for the next eight years making his life hell on earth. Constant arguments and accusations of infidelity motivated him—what?—to marry her in hopes that it would pacify her doubts. Did it work? Perish the thought. When he could stand it no longer and divorced her, she dogged him with myriad accusations and criminal complaints.

Moral of the tale: frigid women are susceptible to hero-worship—as long as the hero keeps his distance—from which distance she can daydream of complete sexual fulfillment in his embrace. But once in bed with her hero, the usual disappointment follows, he is soon transformed from hero to the principal villain.

Thus we have the bait and switch type. It results from wishing for an orgasm, imagining it, but not receiving it. There is another cultural kind as well. We find it in Japanese society. Japanese are known the world over for their politeness. In Japan a stranger is treated like a king, with scrupulous courtesy. As a result of this heritage, a Japanese artist who set up a design shop in Barcelona, asked whether he missed Japan, said he missed the courtesy and the food.

In Barcelona, it's just the opposite. If you are a stranger you are treated indifferently or badly; but as you become better known, you begin to see their good side, or they see yours, or both. But as you become better known to a Japanese, you are treated worse. Instead of perfect manners, you become the brunt of criticism—reserved for family members.

This characteristic of Japan is seen in the domestic dramas of Japanese film director, Yasujiro Ozu (1903–63) whose fifty-four films concentrate on family life. They reveal two things unique to Japan—pertinent to this inquiry. One is the constant criticism of family members by other family members. The other, is that the characters in Ozu's films lack might be described as an "inside."

One learns these unique characteristics from Ozu's films. His characters never talk about themselves, except as one would talk about someone else. In short, characters are not only depicted objectively; they seem to have no subjective side. It results that whatever happened to one of them, someone else was responsible. But criticism balances it out, because everything that happened was, according to other family members, one's own fault.

We see this peculiar trait on an international level. Some Japanese, working in Iraq during the post 9-11 invasion, were taken hostage and held for the better part of a year. When they were finally released and returned to Japan they were not honored or treated as heroes, they were blamed, almost branded, for even being in Iraq and making a stir. And not merely identified as such, but they were called on the telephone at home, work, and leisure by the public, accused of being seriously inconsiderate.

Of course, I didn't know these things when I started to go with a Japanese woman. It started with some small talk in an art session about what we were doing that night. She projected a somewhat bored scenario, which led me to suggest that if she wasn't doing anything else, we might meet later and see a film. She gave a kind of nodding assent, and when, waiting at an oblique angle to the entrance of the theater, I saw her come running not to be late, I thought she might be more interested than she revealed.

After the film, we had a couple of cocktails. Emboldened by her running earlier, by the fact that she didn't have much to say, and by the somewhat amusing idea of just asking on a first date, I suggested we go to my place. I was rather surprised when she replied: "I don't want to play games. I would but I'm on my period, and it's particularly heavy flow."

Actually I don't remember anything else she said that night. I was dating someone else, somewhat casually, so I let a couple of weeks go by before I mentioned her to a mutual friend. He gave me her telephone number, but before I could call her she appeared in the class. She reappeared quite magically, or so it seemed. We went out, and the next night afterwards at my place, she was willing, but not excessively responsive. She was divorced (twice), but she was so enthused and so complimentary. In fact, as I said to a friend of mine, she seemed willing to do anything.

That was how it began. And for a few weeks it continued in this vein. I was the greatest guy in the world, and she seemed determined to please me. She would jump off a bridge if I asked her to, or so it seemed. On a more practical level, she would drive across town to come to my place. She insisted she didn't mind at all. We would find interesting sites, and go landscape drawing together. And make love. And have coffee.

But she had very little to say. And after a few weeks, a reversal gradually began to set in. She was not always available as she once had been. Midweek meetings appeared too time-demanding to handle. Friends, and apparently ex-boyfriends—with whom nothing was now happening, she insisted—would visit her. I wasn't jealous, was I? There was nothing to be jealous about.

To make a long story short, things gradually deteriorated. But she apparently was unaware of it. She mentioned a prenuptial agreement she had discussed with a girlfriend at work, and the topic of marriage was casually introduced into the conversation.

Actually, we were on two different tracks. On one tract, her plans for marriage seemed to be solidifying, with an announcement that she was going celibate for the time being. On the other, my list of grievances was gradually growing: number one being that I couldn't understand how celibacy could be some kind of premarital enticement. But in the surreal world she apparently occupied, her announcement was designed to motivate me to make a serious proposition. As a matter of fact, it had the opposite reaction. It caused a serious fight and an immediate break up of the relationship, which I in any case had long since pronounced doomed.

What was this all about? The pitch and switch of Japanese society was combined with the pitch and switch of a nonorgasmic relationship to produce this absolutely crazy scenario, in which her actions, however implausible to me, seemed perfectly credible to her. Ethnically, the Japanese pitch and switch is weird but not completely incredible. Japanese peasants (in feudal times) could lose their heads quite literally for just being rude to a samurai, I learned from a Japanese–American companion. Thus, their extreme courtesy. The criticism at home stems from the same source: to guard against rudeness outside, criticism inside.

They counterbalance each other in one respect; complement each other in another respect.

Of course, the pitch and switch I am talking about is not basically an cultural device. It is characteristic of a nonorgasmic woman. But they are not totally unrelated. For the Japanese are the least sexually satisfied among industrial nations, according to a recent poll. If the woman is still looking for Mr. Right, you may be the latest candidate. Of course, she will shortly find that you are not right, but wrong, and disappointment begins to set in. You are, alas, just like the rest. Perhaps your assets are stronger, you liabilities less demanding. At least at first, but as time goes by your assets begin to fade and your liabilities become more prominent. You are fading away before your very eyes, without knowing why. In fact, you are not the only one who cannot explain it. She can't either. It's like a bad dream, only you are part of it's demise.

Our purposes, however, are fairly simple. Whether cultural or domestic, pitch and switch is inorgasmic. Hence if your relationship starts to define a declining arc, it's time to jump ship. Pitch and switch might be called—sought but unfulfilled hope.

(v) Hyper-indecision

Pitch and switch (in the last subchapter) suggests a certain premeditation. It may, of course, be more or less automatic—especially, if the reaction is cultural. It may also be somewhat automatic if it is sexually driven. But it may also result from a conscious plotting, strong lead, and weak follow through, gradually drawing you into her mesh. Chronic, hyper-indecision, however, is less deliberate than any of the scenarios discussed so far. Just as women have begun many an embrace with great enthusiasm, only to find themselves high and dry, the pattern of enthusiasm followed by defeating unfulfillment tends to color their entire lives and everything in them.

When Jacqueline Kennedy pointed to this trait as her cardinal moral fault, she probably did not have sex in mind. She was thinking of the quick about face she made concerning other desires and decisions in her life, possibly book deals among other things. It was these other decisions that suffered as a result of her inability to make and keep a total commitment.

Rita Hayworth, as we have noticed, was slated to marry Victor Mature, and almost at the last minute she changed her mind and married Orson Welles. The obvious question here is what this change of mind was really about. The marriage to Welles wasn't her first marriage, so virginal confusion is not in the running as an explanation. Of course, it is virginal confusion in the sense that an inorgasmic woman has never participated in a sexual relationship. She is what the French call a "demi-virge." She is a virgin in her mind, even if not in her body. She has been a victim of sex, but she has never participated.

But there are other interpretations. Philip French, movie critic, in a cameo portrait in *The Observer*, from July 13, 2008, suggests that Rita Hayward was the victim of several men, who were using her fame for their own ends.[1] For her first husband, she was primarily a meal ticket. Orson Welles, on the other hand, wanted her to star in his films. Then Aga Khan wanted her to play a leading role in his real life—bachelor life style. Her last husband, Dick Haymes, thought she might revive his career, and also keep him from being deported.

Victimized by them all—according to French. Plausible enough if you read fast and inattentively, but if you ask one question the case for exploitation crumbles. That question: Where was Rita while all of this was going on? Or to look at the situation from the victimizing man's standpoint, who else did any of Rita's four husbands marry solely for such crass and commercial reasons as French is contending? And who else did they marry for such a short period of time?

The answer is the short duration of her marriages was entirely unique to Rita. And on that basis alone Philip French's rescue operation makes little sense. Rita was married four times; her husbands were not. Orson Wells's third and last marriage to Paola Mori lasted thirty years—from 1955–1985. Rita's last three marriages lasted no longer than three years a piece. The evidence speaks for itself.

Ava Gardner had a similar movie and non-movie career. Married to Mickey Rooney (1942–1943), to Artie Shaw (1945–1947), and to Frank Sinatra (1951–1957), although they were separated in 1954. Roughly two years each. And then she removed to Spain where she attempted to live the life of Hemmingway's *The Sun Also Rises*, the movie version at least, keeping company with rich playboys and matadors, appearing drunk and boisterous, getting thrown out of bars, and barred from others.[2]

To complete our initial trio: Marilyn Monroe is a special case. Let's skip the first marriage and start with the second to baseball player Joe DeMaggio. They were married in 1954, but divorced the same year. In 1956 she began to work in the Actor's studio, then she set up her own studio. She met and married Arthur Miller, for whom she converted to Judaism. The marriage lasted till 1961, although for at least the last two years they were apart.

Marilyn's last film, *The Misfits*, released in 1961, was written by Miller. Nonetheless, or perhaps in part because of his presence, it went far over budget, largely as a direct consequence of her frequent illnesses, overdoses of sleeping pills, mixed with alcoholic drinks.[3]

These biographical notes are not really humorous, although they may seem so. While all these women apparently retained the desire for sexual fulfillment, with the passage of time they became increasingly doubtful that they would ever achieve it. Hence the perennial: Can this be Mr. Right? Hope draws them forward; fear holds them back. When Jackie Kennedy admitted that her "greatest moral fault is that initial enthusiasms tend to fade very quickly," her admission was paradigmatic of the nonorgasmic woman. The result: frozen indecision—on all fronts.

It is not something Jackie really can be blamed for. She was trained to act that way. Like the film *The Manchurian Candidate*, only much earlier and longer in the making, her father, Jack Bouvier "imposed his distinctive view of male–female relations on his daughters." It was simple. Once they gave in, the man was no longer interested. Jack taught Jackie that "a woman's aloofness was a measure of her desirability." He admonished her "never to throw (herself) at anybody, to be reticent and hard to get."[4,5]

Evidently, Jackie learned quite well. Too well. She did not learn how to relax, to let go. And this failure did not end with indecision as to the sex act. It pervaded her life. All her enthusiasms were equally disillusioned. Initial enthusiasms were all turned off before they could develop, and, as she admitted, this was her worst fault. Yet she seemed unable to connect the indecision that stemmed from her sexual incapacity with the rest of her life. Or else she would not have made such a casual but totally revealing statement about herself.

Nor did it end with mere indecision. For indecision puts the mind in a knot. It is an unresolved tension. It must be relieved, or at least its edge must be dulled. Thus we find hyper-indecision leads to chain smoking, or drink, or drugs, or all of them. With Rita Hayworth and Ava Gardner it was drinking. With Marilyn Monroe it was mostly prescription drugs. Working backward, any of these habits, in excess, may be an indication of indecision, and chronic indecision is an indication of an inorgasmic woman. Regular visits to the chiropractor for back strain is another symptom. Why doesn't she stretch? Because stretching is solo, and attention is what she craves. So she makes regular medical appointments for generalized aches and pains which everyone is subject to. It may be called malingering. But with time and repetition it becomes true. She actually becomes sick. The mental habit becomes a physical one.

Indecision means she is afraid of a decision, given her underlying sexual incapacity, because given that incapacity the decision will be wrong either way, either yes or no. Hence she does not wish to make that decision at all. Chronic and debilitating indecision, in a phrase, are a species knowledgeable bachelors must avoid.

(vi) Nothing in Moderation

Directly related to chronic, hyper-indecision is the tendency toward excess and deficiency. If in morals (chapter 3) —the mean is generally best, as Aristotle concludes in his *Nicomachean Ethics*, then a habit of excess is not only ethically misguided, but pragmatically self-destructive.[1] Which is to say, here we experience tendencies toward extremes: promiscuous—around the clock sex—or celibate, with little in between. And we are talking about the same woman! Frantic searches for Mr. Right who she cannot even conceptualize, except in negative terms as overseas or elsewhere, much less find—followed by sullen retreats when the latest candidate fails to break the barrier of her locked, chained, and barricaded dysfunctional door.

Pornophobe or pornophile, she loves sex or can't watch it. But sex is only one extreme. Or the inorgasmic woman may be a blank-staring, wall-flower zombie. She's probably narcissistic, that is, if you're not talking about me, I'm not listening. If she is not a chain smoker, she can't abide the smell of tobacco. As far as kids are concerned, she does not want or particularly like children—that or else it's a house full of kids. Of course, some women stay pregnant in order to give themselves a break from their husband's sexual demands.

The inorgasmic woman either hates animals or has a cathouse (literally)—all neutered and ready to be stuffed. She's either indifferent to the poor or hungry or can't refuse a professional panhandler—proving to you how concerned she is about others. She is either a penny-pincher or a spend-thrift, or both. She spends without limit on clothes. Why? Because she has to get something out of this god-damned marriage, doesn't she? It's not sex or love.

Jackie Kennedy got a $3,000,000 dowry up front from Aristotle Onassis—for herself, and a million for each of her two kids. It wasn't quite voluntary. It was either supply the dowry or give up any claim to use American seaports, according to Bobby Kennedy's biographer. In short, if the ancient Greeks said "Nothing in excess" (*Pan metron ariston*), the nonorgasmic woman says "Nothing in moderation!"

And of course, on the excess side, they tend to spend exorbitant amounts of money, particularly on clothes. Jackie spent thousands of dollars per week on clothes causing the president (John Kennedy) to ask whether she had any idea of the amount she was spending. This, or course, followed the pattern set by his own mother, who we recall, allegedly spent all of her time in church or shopping for clothes. Similarly with Diana, Princess of Edinburg, whose shopping sprees exceeded anyone's imagination.

It is not merely wealthy women, however, whose profligacy is shocking. On a lesser scale, all inorgasmic women tend to be equally spendthrift. Their budgets tend to be promises made but not kept; they are always running over, way over budget. Because what they want this moment, overturns every resolution made to the contrary. They will, they say, figure it out later. But later seems never to come: only the bills, and their intense month end midnight attempt to balance the books.

But it is not only budgets and spending to contend with, a general disdain with all money and what it takes to get it is characteristic. Whether mega or micro, the pattern of excess or deficiency is the same. Actually, they do not like to be questioned as to the whys and wherefores of their actions. Because their actions are emotion driven, not rational or logical, and they rarely come to a good end.

Together with their bizarre conduct, they tend as a consequence to have short or selective memories, and they hate to be criticized for what they do. They may lie to you, but if you catch them and comment on it, they are likely to fly into a rage at you, for making something out of nothing. A personal example: I was dating a girl who said she had stopped smoking. I congratulated her on that decision. Then I found her absenting herself from a gathering to go outside to smoke. I mentioned it to her, expecting a laugh and shrug of the shoulders; but to the contrary, she flew into a rage that I should make a point of such a small thing. Of course, it wasn't the smoking that annoyed me, but her lying about it. To no avail did I propound the difference. She wasn't listening.

In fact, these constant mood swings are characteristic. They can be nice and agreeable as long as things are going as expected. But let some impediment block the way and a violent mood may follow. Probably behind these mood swings, there is a sense of confinement or imprisonment. The sense of being locked up in an unpleasant place creates an urgency to escape. To be sure, the violence of these mood swings is an escape. But the violence itself is sexual.

Strong desire for sexual orgasm pulls a woman strongly in one direction; equally strong frustration pulls them in the opposite direction. Since fulfillment must be as strong as the desire, and its frustration as keenly felt as the blocked desire, the emotion finds its expression in these alternating moods and reactions.

So, at least, Wilhelm Reich teaches. Such women are too calm and undisturbed when they are calm, and too violent when they are not. In Francois Truffaut's film *The Man Who Loved Women*, we see the perfect example of such a woman—though not identified as such. The protagonist—in Truffaut's film—encounters such a woman in a restaurant, as I have related. Married to a doctor, but whose flirtatious nature continuously overcomes her conservative decisions. When he follows her and her husband from the restaurant (where their encounter began) to their apartment, he finds her number on the car windshield, and calls her. She registers shock, but nonetheless meets him in the hallway to find out what his call is about. Not wanting to talk on the staircase, they go down to his car, merely not to be seen by neighbors, and then agrees to go to his house simply to discuss the situation. On the way she asks his horoscope sign, but finding it is very bad for her, she demands that they return to her apartment. Now in the garage, a neighbor enters, and not to be seen she puts her face in his lap. When he neighbor leaves the garage, she insists that she didn't see him in the restaurant, but changes her story, and admits that she did. And then, in a complete reversal, she is on top of him.[2]

In his reminiscence after subsequent assignations, these positive decisions and negative reversals are continuous. Later in the story, he asks her to go to his apartment but she refuses because he must have had dozens of assignations with women in that apartment; but then she decides to go, only to complain that she will not sit on his sofa, where many of his assignations must have occurred. Pacified however, she stays, but in the morning when she finds him reading a book, which she decides is just to ignore her, she seizes the book from his hands and throws it out the window so he must to run three floors to the street to retrieve it.

These continuous reversals are doubtless plot driven to keep the audience on edge, but beneath such stylistic features, a self-opposing personality type emerges in which every first conservative impulse is met and opposed by a radical replacement. These opposing redundancies are fed by sexual impulses that pull in one direction, are repelled and must find another outlet. The substitute turns out to be a superficial outlet, sufficient to absorb the physical energy invested, but insufficient to satisfy the sexual energy involved.

The problem with all the exaggerated behavior is generally the same. Freud calls it sublimation. It is an attempt to substitute one kind of behavior for another. Sexual satisfaction is desired but unavailable due to social training. Substitutes are sought, but are all unsatisfactory. The volume is turned up, but still is unsatisfactory. So it's "up, up and away." The woman's behavior in this case is obviously that of an inorgasmic female seeking relief from an unsatisfactory marriage, but is not dealt with in such a way as to show this circumstance, but to depict her as a kind of adventurous, seeking the satisfaction that an adventure may supply. Denying her this, her conduct becomes a bizarre recitation of improbabilities, proving the author did not know what he was dealing with. Female probabilities are not male probabilities. This is the lesson to be learned from Francois Truffaut's *The Man Who Loved Women*.

To which we should add Aristotle's concurrence in the *Poetics*, that in a tragedy, a woman should not have the attributes of a man unless she is a goddess, as in Euripidies' *Medea*, where Medea kills her two children and when her husband comes to revenge himself, she escapes in a magic chariot supplied by an acknowledged god. [3] But the wider lesson for our attentive bachelor is that behavior which is inappropriate for a male may be entirely appropriate for a female, and he must scale his anticipations accordingly.

(vii) "Let's Be Friends"

"Let's be friends" is not so much an invitation, as it is a warning. It's high testosterone talking. Not caring for—rejecting might be closer—the role of female, she may yearn for the apparent independence of the male. Hence she tends to go out for male occupations (engineering, law, medicine, business), and male sports (karate, hunting, fishing, camping, baseball).

Notice how many Olympic female contenders have boy's bodies, with broad shoulders and slim hips; as opposed to the average female with slim shoulders and broad hips. It makes one wonder whether Olympic athletes should not be scored on the basis of testosterone counts, rather than crudely as "male" and "female."

But in terms of gender and dating, one must notice whether she prefers men's clothing, short hair to bald, and she will drive the car. In sex she prefers to be on top. Antithetically, she prefers fellatio to intercourse (she's in control of both you and herself)—but as a matter of fact, she can't tonight because she's too tired; or she has to get up early; or she has a headache (migraines = fire alarm symptom!); backaches are typical; or her yeast infection requires medication which, alas, rules out sex, it will wake the children; and countless other bodily complaints, ailments, and off putting conditions.

Even the phrase "let's be friends" is a warning sign. It's useless for the male to respond: But I don't need female friends, especially females who want to be friends, but who, nevertheless, want to be called and opportuned with invitations. She has already identified herself as inorgasmic by putting the dating proposal in these words, and conversation past this point merely passes the time, until the real thing comes along—if you are lucky, and she does come along.

"I have many boyfriends," she is apt to brag. Why? Because they actually are boyfriends, and not lovers, or they soon will be demoted to just being friends. As I previously mentioned, Ernest Hemmingway's third wife, Martha Gellhorn tells in her bio that she just went along with the program, and by implication, sexual relations with many and sundry men, adopting the freshman congressional motto to another purpose, "You have to go along, to get along." But sex was just for openers, and they were soon expected to settle down to being, in fact, just friends.

A personal case: I had the fortune, or misfortune, to meet one such female. Sex was fine when we first met, but it was shortly withdrawn, hesitantly, and an offer of friendship was made in its place. In vain did I point out that I have enough friends in my own neighborhood, and I could hardly see driving across town if that is what is offered. This was her method—friendship—and nothing I said was going to change it. In fact, I couldn't understand how I got sucked into having this conversation at all.

"My husband used to go hunting for a week in season," she recounted with a smile. "I didn't mind. It gave me the chance to catch up on some things of my own." She told this story, as a kind of paradigm of marital bliss. Actually, it was just the opposite. She was happy as hell to be rid of him. The story should have been post scripted with a message to the effect: "Stay as long as you like."

That was her second husband, who became her second divorce, when she decided to sleep by herself in the basement. Sometime later, after we parted, she met a guy online, who lived in South Africa. They wrote to one another for a period of time. He invited her to come to South Africa. Believe it or not, after almost a year of correspondence she did go, advising her ex-husband that she might be getting married to this man, in which case she might not come back.

Accordingly they made some kind of arrangements for the kids. When she went to South Africa, it turned out that they each put their better self (who I wish I was) on paper, and what was on their paper—actually internet—prospectus was not the reality of their lives. Doubtless, the reality overwhelmed them, and they politely thought that maybe they should think it over more carefully, before proceeding further.

The point to the story is how unreal the suggestion "let's be friends," can be. It can mean a lot of different things, but one thing it always means is: "Let's leave sex on the backburner."

Another personal case: I met a doctor and asked her to go swimming. She consented, but then overslept. Try again. They were having some kind of medical consultation at the hospital, so we met afterward at a bar in my neighborhood around nine o'clock. But to my surprise, she arrives at the bar rather dressed up. How come? That's the way they dress for these things. We have a drink. She doesn't want another. What to do? "Let's go to your place and see your art," she suggests. Fine, I thought, things are proceeding; but then she throws in, as a kind of afterthought: "Let's be friends, OK?"

Now I am slightly confused, what kind of "friends" is she talking about? In other words, is sex included, or not included in her definition? We go to my house, I show her some paintings. Perhaps she would like to watch a film. I was particularly amused by the British television series, *The Singing Detective*, particularly the part where the nurse is washing the patient's (the Detective's) entire body, and he cannot control himself.[1] That gets a laugh from her. We talk. And she makes no move to go. If she makes a move, even a gesture in a familiar direction, I will pick up on it. But no, she doesn't do anything but sit there.

Was she willing? I have no idea. I asked her, what was the business about being friends. She said men get so offended when you drop them, she didn't want that to happen again. That doesn't sound like friends. If it were friends, dumping should not be a concern. So there you have the ambiguity. What is not ambiguous is what kind of a relationship it would be. It's called blind man's bluff. She holds all the cards, and you can guess what she has.

(viii) Delinquent Dads

Bad, absent, oppressive or spineless dads are a very strong counter-indication for sexual fulfillment in a relationship with the daughters of these fathers with the characteristics described. The situation is almost as bad as with two-time losers. Actually, they are close to one another. For the latter almost invariably has some of the characteristics of delinquent dads. Why? Because dad provides the paradigm in a male-female relationship, and if that was a downer, there is little hope for a new paradigm supplanting the earlier one.

We must take a moment to explain that these separate topics are not categorically distinct or separate. A woman (or man in some cases) might be placed in several different categories of dysfunction. In fact, the more we know about her, the more her inorgasmic symptoms will reappear in several contexts.

The question is this: ask about dad. If she bad-mouths him, and throws in her ex-husband to boot—make no mistake—you are the next target on this conveyor belt of criticism. Listen closely and you will learn what shortly she is going to be saying about you.

To schematize the problem, bad dads may be placed either one or the other of two dialectically opposite kinds. Either he is always there at home controlling every aspect of her life, or he is never there and has nothing to do with her. Obviously, we can place an infinite number of different kinds between these two extremes, but for simplicity let us place a third kind in the center: one who is around just enough to be irritating, the one who has numerous concerns, but cannot translate them into any kind of consistent policy.

For the first division, we might nominate Hillary Clinton or Barbara Walter's dad, both of whom were always home.[1] In Hillary's case, according to Carl Bernstein, he was hypercritical. And being hypercritical, his comments were soon rejected and he was personally rejected along with his advice. With Barbara Walter's dad, he was "a kind of poet who read all the time, seemed to live in his own head, and had a hard time showing affection." She never or rarely had any physical contact with him. As a result, his comments and criticisms were also rejected.[2]

With both Barbara Walters and Hillary Clinton, we have bad dads. Of course, we cannot talk about dad without talking about his other half. How dad gets along with the woman of the house is crucial. If she continuously puts him down, he has a big problem. A remark here, a remark there, and what defense does he have? This is the situation in which frigid mothers breed frigid wives. The biggest problem is that dad rarely sees the big picture. He rarely sees that his wife's constant or even occasional remarks eventually add up to a constant brand. In fact, many criticisms may be made, sotto voce, when the father is not present or without hearing.

"He rarely helps around the house," is a favorite. Or, "He takes little interest in the children," is another. Both of these comments are chapter and verse for Barbara Walters. "He's too much of a disciplinarian." This applies to Hillary Clinton's father. If all of his vices—and we all have vices—are constantly in the foreground, and virtues are rarely if ever mentioned, at this rate dad is going to wind up a villain or a nonentity. This tends to be what the inorgasmic wife either consciously or unconsciously wants. It neutralizes dad, and makes him an unwanted visitor in his home.

With a missing father, a woman simply has no male figure in her life, and no male paradigm to relate to. If she has a brother she was close to, an older brother, in particular, there may be an exception to this rule. He may supply the missing element in the paradigm: he may provide the model for a male-female relationship.

This roundabout brings us to the question of the ideal male-female relationship. Women sometimes complain that men do not want to move away from mom, who frequently provides everything they need: shelter, food, and love. They become mama's boys, according to this criticism, which the *New York Times* columnist Maureen Dowd has made.[3]

Actually, the criticism is not quite justified. The ideal relationship, between a man and a woman, is one in which the man in a woman's life is not only her lover, but her father and brother as well. As a lover he may be jealous and possessive; but as a father he may be more interested in her general well-being; while as a brother he may take a more detached view of her problems and interests. She needs all three, if it can be managed.

Similarly with a man, he needs not only a lover, but a mother, and a sister as well: a mother to take care of him, a sister to give him good advice as to his dealings with others, and a lover to deal with the here and now.

So in fact, both men and women need all three relationships. If only it could be managed. Actually, then, it's not just dad who needs scrutiny. The nature of a woman's entire home life needs examination.

(ix) Mindful Moms

Any positive views of a man must be immediately squelched by the bad experiences her mother had with her marital partners. How could their daughter extricate herself from these continuously negative appraisals?

But the problems with men and women in marriage go deeper than this. Men and women are different, even if the whole tendency of modern society is to treat them as if they were equal. Equal pay for equal work says President Obama. But there is no equal work. Everyone does a job differently and every difference is a difference in quality. I am not against equal pay, I am against putting it under a banner which makes little sense on examination.

What are the differences between males and females? Even in embryo, the differences are apparent. If the child starts kicking in the middle of the night, there is already an indication that the infant is a male, showing that the male is more active than the female. After birth, we find that the female has pulled ahead in grammar and must wait several years for the male to catch up. But the question is rarely or never asked, what was the male doing while the female was involved in grammar? He was involved in gravitational studies—running, jumping, climbing, throwing balls, wrestling, and all such activities.

It is rarely noticed that the study of grammar is mostly directed toward the past and the study of gravity is mostly directed at the present. We can see this in the newspapers—the sporting page occupies men, while the style page occupies women. But this is not the most important difference, there is a diagrammatic difference in the way men and women confront a problem. Women are more likely to address a problem from the bottom up, while men address the problem from the top down. We can see this in the 2016 presidential race with Hillary Clinton, Bernie Sanders, and Donald Trump.

Former president Bill Clinton tended to salute his wife's capacities by saying that if Hillary Clinton was brought into a problematic situation, when she left, it would be improved by her efforts. How, what, when, where, to what extent—he did not say. His remarks exemplify the trait she is best known for—it exemplifies the bottom up approach to a problem.

Bernie Sanders on the other hand, exemplifies the top down approach. The most serious problem facing the planet is global warming, according to his statement. The next most serious problem on the planet is the radical disproportion in the distortion of income and assets. This dramatic difference in the way problems are approached, marks a very serious difference between men and women in confronting any problem. Female orgasm is one such problem. Women largely follow Hillary's advice of "faking it until you can make it" if there are sexual problems. And they become disappointed and baffled when this method eventually wears thin and then wears out as a way of solving marital difficulties. Fake it until you can make it doesn't work as a solution, according to the sex researchers, Masters and Johnston. For the woman soon feels like she is a sex slave which indeed she is when the solution turns from annoyance and discomfort to positive hatred. The best advice is to avoid the problem altogether.

If the lady in question comes from a happy home, there's a good chance your home will be happy also; if not, problems from her upbringing will bleed over into your life. In other words, time invested in getting to know her family will be well rewarded.

Imagine your wife as her mother. It's an exercise well spent, because to an extent you cannot imagine that at present, she is going to become her mother. Sooner than you think, say ten years, she is going to undergo a transformation. Then to your astonishment, you will suddenly find your mother-in-law where you expected to find your wife.

Now look at her mother's relation with her husband. Often this is plain enough. They get on quite well with each other. Fine! An important hurdle has been overcome. But consider the opposite situation. They are separated and their relationship is terrible. If your female friend echoes her mother's view of her dad, then there is no real point in continuing the relationship—at least on a serious basis. It really doesn't matter whether what she says is true or false, it's the relationship that counts: if mom says he is a loser, not only him but all men are similarly deficient.

In between these two extreme possibilities, there is a world of possible relationships to define. It's perplexing, not only to you, but possibly to her as well. The question needs to be pursued until you have a definite view of things, because this relationship with her dad is going to be your relationship with her before long. So this is a relationship you must look at long and hard—for she is going to become her mother, and you are going to become her father, at least in the hard-core situation you must deal with—baring other traumas which may cloud your life.

The fact is, there are a million marital scenarios, and you must be prepared to see clearly what is going on if you do not wish to get caught up in the cross-fire of one of them. What did I do? You may ask yourself when your wife is in a bad mood. Often times it is nothing you did which sets her mood. It is something which falls into a domestic pattern that triggered a generic response. In other words, you are being punished for something your wife's father did to her mother. This is why people frequently get on quite well when they are single, and things change when they get married.

Thus did Hillary's mom divorce her dad. Thus is Hillary living separately from Bill. Divorce is a kind of family heirloom, passed from one generation to the next. Take Alice—a pseudonym for an actual model in my art sessions—for example. Everything casually seemed to be in place in her life. For one thing, she had a marvelous figure. Quite good looking as well. A major in philosophy. A seeming gift from the gods. But on more familiar terms, this picture began to break down. She was married, but oddly, she slept in her own bedroom. "The door's open," she said. "Anyone can come in."

The key to the situation eventually turned out to be that her mother was married and divorced three times. And the third time—when Alice was a child—was the last. Learning this ended my interest at the threshold. Alice, in turn, had numerous petty complaints about her husband. When she talked about him, one wondered what kept this marriage going.

As a matter of fact, I was not surprised when her husband asked me one day if I handled divorces. The answer was yes, but I didn't want to handle his—not unless it was a case of leaving with the clothes on your back—which it wasn't.

With a mother divorced three times, there is a terrible weight placed upon the shoulders of a woman brought up in that household. Imagine the conversation. Then imagine what that conversation does to a woman's desire for a man. The point is, the greater your familiarity with the family from which your female interest emerged, the better your chance for an enduring relationship. The relationship starts will you dating a particular female that you believe to be an individual, with an individual will, and the family doesn't count for much. Perish the thought.

(x) Post Coitum

Or after-sex-blues. The Latin phrase is *Post Coitum Tutti Animali Triste*, after sex all animals are sad.[1] This obviously is not what we believe in America today. Today it might read *Post Coitum Tutti Animali Felix*, after sex all animals are happy. But of course neither of these generalizations are true. Sex is rarely perfect. And to a certain extent what makes you happy or sad is a matter of training. In France for example most people register themselves in general as sad as compared with America where most say they are happy. Is there much difference in happiness from country to country? We are to some extent schooled to talk about our situation differently. But early training also makes a difference in attitude.

As far a a as happiness, taken by country, recent surveys show surprising differences. The happiest country in the industrialized world, appears to be Denmark, the saddest is Japan. If we asked why this is so, sex appears to be a large part of the answer. In Japan, the passive submissiveness of women results in their unhappiness in sex, where they are supposed to satisfy the man, and not to say no to their husbands. They become the vessel of his "happy" sexual experience.

In Denmark on the other hand, you probably have the closest sexual equality in the industrialized world. Not only premarital equality, but marital equality as well. The result is equality of sexual satisfaction, and happiness seems strongly tied to that. Of course, that's not all, political freedom and freedom of expression follows, or comes hand in hand with sexual freedom. Probably the closest to real democracy in the western world next to Switzerland. Happiness seems to follow from the generality of these conditions.

So it is probably the case that sexual freedom goes a long way toward establishing the conditions of a happy life. Just as, the opposite extreme, sexual inhibition seems to set the stage for an unhappy life.

Martha Gellhorn is a good example. Hemingway's third wife, you will remember. Her father had imparted mixed messages, according to Gellhorn's biographer; Caroline Moorehead.[2] It was guilt if you refused, shame if you accepted. This was a fear that Martha had with her first sexual experience. As a consequence, it was an experience that she neither wanted nor enjoyed. Evidentially, there was something wrong with her, she reasoned. She was "not quite a woman." Hence she fled, packing her knapsack and crawling out of a window. "Embarrassed in a way that was so profound," she later recounted, "that I doubt if I can ever describe it."

Perhaps like Meg Ryan in the film *When Hally Met Sally*, Martha learned to fake an orgasm, but she couldn't and probably didn't see the need to try to fake the psychological relaxation which normally follows.[3] After sex, a nonorgasmic woman is restless, she wants to do something besides lie there—not because she is bored, but because she is highly agitated. That something else usually turns out to be picking a fight about some unrelated topic, one of an infinite number of her companion's habitual ways of disregarding her expectations and/or sensitivities.

If you want to know how the woman feels without an orgasm, try *Coitus Interrupts* (sex without orgasm), not once, but repeatedly, without the relief of even an occasional orgasm, and you will be able to empathize with your companion. And because she didn't have an orgasm with you, she is still looking, flirting, and jumping into bed with any likely or unlikely candidate. If you suspect she is cheating, she might be—in spirit at least, if not in body.

As time goes by, you experience a gradual come-down in your companion's opinion. Your virtues, such as they may be, seem less significant. And your vices, which we all have, are more numerous and extensive than they formally seemed to be. We are into the pitch and switch mood, except that there may be no pitch here, merely a let-down from failure to find relief in orgasm. There may be no high opinion to descent from. Merely confirmation of an already low opinion of the male of the species.

Charlie Chaplin, in his autobiography, says that he is not disposed to dwell on such matters, but he tells us enough to see that most of his affairs were with women whom Cybill Shepherd described in her interview with Dick Cavett, when she said: "You know what they say in Hollywood, the men are less than men, and the women are more than women." This was true at least until Chaplin's final marriage to Oona O'Neill, where he appears to have married a winner.[4]

In Hollywood, as Cybill Shepherd advises, the odds are even worse than in the general population, whatever that is. Models and actors at least, must be free and easy about sex, it would seem. Actually, Shepherd's observation applies with special force to entertainers and models. The nudity of art models for instance, seems like the gateway to more intimate relations, and this turns out to be closed till further notice.

Nudity is not a prelude to something else, as you may surmise, but the whole show. Nude modeling is not a prelude, it is a substitute. It is what women do who have a nice body, but really are not motivated, and don't see the point in sharing it with anyone else. Women for whom sex is part of the performing arts, tend to be nonorgasmic. Whereas, women who are orgasmic, tend less to want to show sex off. This is a generalization with notable exceptions, which do not provide a rule to guide a man's conduct. The one rule that can be followed, is that the woman who is relaxed post coitum is generally orgasmic, whereas the woman who seeks activity is suspect to be seeking something else.

But to return to the main topic of this section, which is the aftermath of sexual relations, the general reaction of orgasmic women is to seek relaxation, while with the nonorgasmic woman, the desire is for activity. Thus Ava Gardner's statement that "arguments started on the way to the bidet," is as revealing that no orgasm occurred as Marilyn Monroe's statement that she never had an orgasm. While for Rita Hayworth, her alcoholism, tantrums, hospitalizations, and five marriage rules her out as a possibility for orgasm. One key indicator that is often unappreciated by nonorgasmic women who believe that their actions are sufficient to convince, when in fact their post coitum actions, uninformed by this knowledge, are just as convincing. In the film *When Harry Met Sally*, the whole adventure was in the performance of the orgasm, and there was no inquiry into the aftermath, which is the most revealing. This is where a knowledgeable man will see at a distance the difference and know what to make of it.

CHAPTER 6
Bio-Psycho-Social Factors

(a) The Greatest Pleasure

"Sexuality, a complex phenomena, can be responsible for the greatest pleasure and deepest pain known to man," states Nancy Fugate Woods, author of *Human Sexuality in Health and Illness*.[1]

Author and intellectual Susan Sontag has given an even more explicit and expansive reason. "The coming of orgasm has changed my life," she relates. "I am liberated, but that's not the way to say it...sexuality is a paradigm...the orgasm focuses, I need to write the coming orgasm is not the solution, but, more the birth of my eye." *London Review of Books* (February 17, 2009).[2]

More recently Naomi Wolf has come out with *Vagina: A New Biography* in which she asserts that the vagina, properly understood, is "part of the female soul," hence part of the "meaning of life itself."[3] Ms. Wolf had the disabling experience of being deprived of her ability to have a vaginal orgasm, and this in turn, vacated her life of all "the light and sparkle of the world." Eventually consulting her gynecologist, she learned that there was a misalignment of her spinal column, causing a compression of her pelvic nerve, and this in turn, a partial sexual insensitivity. Corrected by surgery, her vaginal orgasms returned, and with them that certain perfection in the unity and purpose of her life.

Zoe Heller, reviewing Wolf's *Biography*, for *The New York Review of Books*, picks away at contradictory details of Wolf's message; without realizing that her review itself is subject to the same critique—which incline one to believe that critics should be candid enough to include a statement—such as one finds in financial papers—of their own sexual history and responsiveness.[4]

Certainly a nonorgasmic woman cannot deal dispassionately with a memoir as passionate as Ms. Wolf's. Such a critic's response to Wolf's work is likely to contain a second phantom personality: the critic herself, whose every statement about Wolf's excessive enthusiasm, contains an implied admission of the critic's less enthusiastic participation in her own sex life.

In any case, it is curious, that the single decision in a man's life most likely to lay the foundation for a happy life, or for long-term misery, receives almost no attention in the modern family, or in schools, or in the media, or simply in conversation between men.

To fill the gap, this book deals with how to avoid a doomed relationship and to know that most heterosexual divorces occur in the fourth or fifth year of marriage. A female commentator on sex and marriage theorizes that after four or five years serotonin levels drop and sexual satisfaction drops with it. If the marriage was based solely or mainly on sex, the marriage collapses with the collapse of the sexual relationship.

A somewhat related theory is that testosterone and serotonin are contrary indicators: when one's serotonin level stops, testosterone elevates. According to this theory serotonin governs one's sex drive: testosterone governs love and friendship. Give four or five years for thriving sex, if the marriage ends about this time, the indication is that it laced the testosterone necessary to furnish the basis for a marriage based on friendship.

Whichever explanation one prefers, a statistic published a few years ago noticed that while men tend to be happier in their second marriages than in their first, a high percentage of women find no real improvement the second time around. This is something for men seriously to consider, the inference being that the woman's discontent is not caused by Tom, Dick or Harry: a regular relation with any man is at it's core. Her discontent is not quite conscious usually not deliberate; to an extent it's an unconscious mood, forcing her feelings and consequent actions.

Sometimes women learn their unsuitability for marriage after two or three tries. Then their dislike for the institution becomes more or less apparent to them. This was the case with Barbara Walters, according to her biography, as we have seen. After the second try she knew that marriage was not for her. But she went on, for a third try, which ended like the first two.

These second and third marriages are almost all cases of inability to have an orgasm. "Why should you care?" a woman recently asked me. Orgasm serves no evolutionary function, she insisted. But another source, another opinion: this one insists that orgasm does serve a function, for satisfaction in sex promotes retention of the sperm, and this facilitates pregnancy.

But, of course having a child is not the focus of this inquiry. The question is how to build a happy relationship—and the role of an orgasm in that relationship. The position taken here is that orgasm is necessary for a harmonious and happy relationship. It is vital for men pursuing a woman to be fully cognizant of this fact.

(b) Sexual Progress/Regress

Stimulated by the highly publicized but now-resolved charges of sexual misconduct against French politician Dominique Strauss-Kahn, an American journalist at the time, Feifei Sun, devised and published "The Misconduct Matrix," which schematized charges against nineteen allegedly sexually misbehaving men into four categories. In the first division—top to bottom—"Massively Hypocritical," philanderers were separated from "Just Plain Stupid," deviants. And—from left to right—those who made "Doghouse" mistakes, were separated from those who broke the law and were placed in the "Jailhouse," category.[1]

Reading the captions allegedly describing the activities of these philandering men inclines one to think that there should be a special category for Sun—like mud-slinging journalist extraordinaire. I should like to have him on the witness stand to ask a few questions, like: What is your basis for condemning Woody Allen? Was it for taking a nude picture of Soon-Yi, as you state? Did you place him in the Doghouse, and called him Just Plain Stupid for that?

And Thomas Jefferson, who you also placed in the Doghouse category—only in the "Massively Hypocritical" part of that category—with no conclusive evidence as to his sex life at all. Similarly, for now-past Senator John Edwards, his wife was incapacitated with cancer. With Arnold Schwarzenegger, not enough is known to condemn him, nor do we know enough about Eliot Spitzer, or John Ensign, or Gary Hart. Nonetheless, what we do know is here you have what are called "charges" and nothing more. Isn't a person innocent until proven guilty in this country? Indeed, only two out of nineteen have been proven guilty of anything. Mike Tyson was convicted of rape, and Larry Craig of disorderly conduct.

Obviously it would be politically incorrect to defend all these accused men by pointing to their possibly frigid wives as a precipitating cause of their sexual alienation from the marriage. Nonetheless if you are going to treat the topic at all, a concern for elementary fairness dictates some mention of causation.

From the standpoint of the Christian right sexual intercourse is sinful and permitted for procreation only. So for readers of this persuasion, such editorial balance is not at all necessary. The deed is self-enclosed.

In the midst of this reportage I was mildly shocked to hear a commentator remark: "I think Hillary has some explaining to do." My thought exactly! Unfortunately, his idea was a voice in the wilderness. As far as the mainstream media was concerned, Hillary did not need to explain anything, except perhaps why she stayed with philandering Bill.

The underlying but unmentioned fact is in the United States at least we are living in a Neo-Victorian era, produced this time by the feminist lobby, aided by a warped media. And it is not only the lobby, but in the last thirty years, women have taken a job description most men would as soon avoid—as gatekeepers—in the process becoming sexual guardians for the mainstream media. One result is the relative scarcity of public discussions of failed orgasm as the cause of so-called philandering by the men involved.

Thus, for example, one notes the absence of "orgasm" from the topics treated in Dr. Robert M. Goldenson's magisterial two-volume *The Encyclopedia of Human Behaviour*. Dealing with Sigmund Freud's former associate, Willem Reich, Dr. Goldenson treats Reich as a quack whose "fanciful" theories failed to take into account the "well-known" fact "that many highly disturbed individuals are still capable of full orgasmic potency."[2]

Indeed Reich nowhere claimed that disturbed individuals are incapable of orgasm. His argument ran in the other direction: his claim being that individuals who did not experience orgasm exhibited neu-rotic anxieties—not the reverse, that one could not experience orgasm, if one was neurotic. In any case, potency is defined as potential and not performance, and Reich was concerned with converting the former—potential—into performance. No, Reich's offense was more basic. He went further than anyone else to disturb the apple cart of equal sexual opportunity. The reason doesn't matter.

More recently, is *Sex at Dawn: The Prehistoric Origins of Modern Sexuality*, by Christoper Ryan and Cacilda Jetha, who write that sex re-lations as we know them today is not "natural." In fact, monogamous relations were not vigorously prescribed until the advent of agricultural societies—before which societies were far more egalitarian and open to changing relationships. With the rise of agriculture comes the institution of class, and with this change comes the strict repression of polygamous relationships.[3]

But of course, repression of sexuality means heterosexual coupling, not the "message" practiced by doctors to relieve—by orgasm—symptoms of hysteria, such as "anxiety, sleeplessness, irritability, nervousness" and "erotic fantasies," for which we, in the late Nineteenth Century became "the largest single market for therapeutic services."

Accordingly debunked by Ryan and Jetha, is the somewhat popular notion that women are naturally less sexual than men. And with it the *New York Times'* one-third, one-third, one-third taxonomy with which we began. This division of sexual satisfaction, it now clearly appears, is not biological or natural, but conditioned by the class structure of soci-ety. It is a perversion which Wilhelm Reich rejects.[4]

It is also a position that squares with a biological view of man in nature. For of the nearly five thousand species of mammals, only about 4 percent stay with one mate for life—according to *The Guardian Weekly* (2012). So man, freed from his class structure of sexual repression—or unmindful of it—might join the 4,800 species of mammals which do not attempt to scale the Mount Everest of sexual monogamy, and join those whose idea of sexual equality carries with it a more liberated idea of sexual association—free from the journalistic condemnation of Feifei Sun, with whose article we began this section.[5]

(c) The Misleading Media

In an article in the *Guardian*, October 20, 2010, John Pilger states: "If people really knew the truth, the war would be stopped tomorrow.[1] But of course, they don't know, and can't know." They can't know because the truth about the war is not being reported.

But it is not only news about the war that is distorted by the media. All the news reported by mainstream media is bent and twisted—it it's reported at all—in the sacred cause of making money. What would the news be like, if it was not controlled by mainstream media? Thomas Jefferson insisted that democracy depends on "free flowing information." But where do we find that rare resource? We did not have it during the Vietnam war, and we do not have it now, in Middle East conflicts.

In his book *Propaganda* (1928), Edward Bernays, describes his subject as "an invisible government that is the true ruling power in our country."[2] The press does not tell the masses what they can do; it tells them what to think. Hence the power that controls the media controls the masses.

The point, however, is that the masses are not merely manipulated about war and politics, they are manipulated about everything else as well. In reference to our topic, female orgasm, the French director Jean-Luc Godard criticized Francois Truffaut for concentrating on love or sexuality and neglecting politics. In response to which Truffaut stated that he saw more truth (and falsity) in the bedroom than in the boardroom.

Consider, for example, the opposite side of Feifei Sun's article (called "The Misconduct Matrix.[3] Let's interview nineteen women, on better evidence, for unresponsiveness, and write suitable descriptions of their domestic life as the basic cause of marital breakups. Can anyone imagine such an essay being published in a popular magazine in America? It is unimaginable. Editors would begin howling before you reached the second sentence of your presentation.

There is no discussion of what happens, or does not happen, in marital bedrooms, which might provide the motive for a male searching for sexual satisfaction elsewhere. We never hear of the frigidity of Hemmingway's wives. We never or rarely hear of the discussion of divorce between Jack and Jacqueline Kennedy, before he decided to run for president. We never hear of the sexual side of Kennedy's father's relationship with six-time loser Gloria Swanson. Or of Frank Sinatra's bedroom farce with Ava Gardner, who spent her time attempting to escape his clutches—and his sexual desires. There is virtually nothing in print on these subjects that I have discovered. Or finally, of Woody Allen's apparent reluctance to move from his apartment and share a living space with Mia Farrow. Why are all these newsworthy topics never or rarely mentioned in mainstream media?

The answer is obvious: they are never or rarely mentioned because there is a publishing code that prohibits bringing these topics to the fore. Nancy Fugate Woods, in her article on human sexuality: "35% never reached orgasm during the first year of marriage." (p. 15) How could this topic of female frigidity avoid extensive media coverage, especially, considering that male "philandering" subject receives such a constant and unexplained spread?[4]

Arthur Miller's marriage to Marilyn Monroe is an example of extreme media distortion. He has the temerity to complain that his marriage to Marilyn Monroe cost him to lose more than five years of his life, during which time he couldn't work or do anything else. (Think what you will of his work. I place him middlebrow, according to Dwight Macdonald's now ancient scheme.) Miller wrote a book about his marriage to Marilyn and gave an interview to *Vanity Fair*. I skimmed the book and read the interview. The result? I have no real idea of what the fuss was about.[5]

The story goes that she threatened if Bobby Kennedy continued to ignore her calls, she would go public with the story of how the Kennedy men had used her. On the known facts this is a story going nowhere, so writers threw in her semi-incoherent threats, to raise the question of whether there was not foul play in her apparent suicide. But questions are not proof. All we know is that the plot invented by journalists is so attenuated it is almost impossible to follow, much less to believe.

The point I am making, however, is this: frigid or nonorgasmic women are the subspecies (of our initial three) most likely to complain of being used and abused; and men, either simply wary of media bashing, or even possibly from more traditional notions of gentlemanly behavior, decline to challenge the frustrated female version of the facts. Almost all the notables previously mentioned as philanders eventually gave up on finding anything at home, and wound up with other women—alas, frequently also frigid. Then they accept social condemnation, rather than reveal the marital fraud perpetrated by their cold and unresponsive wives.

The situation is not restricted to women, however. On the male side we might include the case of philosopher Paul Feyerabend, who, as a German soldier, was shot in the spine during World War II. He was rendered impotent. Nonetheless he learned how to satisfy the women he dated, and was married four times. The problem was the same as with nonorgasmic women. He could satisfy them, but not himself.

After a short while, he began to feel like a prisoner with the result that "I practically lived in my study or my office writing 'important papers.'" I was often in love, he relates, but it was mostly a matter of imagination, which fizzled when it became real. In short, the same scenario as with the nonorgasmic women, love failed when the promise of sex was permanently unfulfilled.

Wilhelm Reich's books had a strong point. And that point is that a lot of what is wrong with contemporary society is found in what is wrong in the bedroom of sexually unsatisfied marriages. Sexual incompatibility is the cause of several of the largest industries in modern society—divorce among them. When you consider that "Sexual maladjustment was found to be a contributing cause in the failure of about three fourths of upper-class marriages that ended in separation or divorce" (p. 14), you begin to realize the ubiquitous impact of sexual maladjustment on society.[6]

A glance at Hemmingway's several wives, Brando's Anna Kashfi, Picasso's Francise Gilot—a sample of nonorgasmic affection: a certain characteristic reserves; cloaks that continuous watch and wait for their prey to drop his guard—that one typically encounters in carnivores.

The conclusion is well-nigh inescapable, and it runs counter to mainstream media's favorite myth: that a woman's sexual responsiveness, or lack thereof, is a matter of habit, which can be reformed. Habit yes, but better described as hard-core wiring tenaciously resistant to change. The older the woman—or man for that matter—the more resistant to change she or he becomes. It is therefore a matter of the utmost importance that one who seeks happiness in their relations with the opposite sex be able to identify which of the three subspecies he or she has in hand, whether orgasmic, nonorgasmic, or irregular or periodically responsive, and to banish from one's mind the improbable suggestion, so frequently encountered in popular magazines, that patience and technique may change things. They may, but it is highly unlikely.

(d) Why Do So Many Rich and Famous Men...?

To repeat Fanny Brice's rhetorical question: "Why do so many rich and famous men marry frigid women?" Her answer to that question: "Because they are such good actresses!" This provides a terse but accurate picture of the situation. In other words, men are duped into believing that these actresses (lay and professional) that they married enjoy sex as much as they do, only to find, after the ceremony that it was an act.

Of course, having stated that fact implies another equally true explanation: men are stupid, unimaginative, insensitive, or socially conditioned, to be so easily duped. Hillary Clinton (as we have seen) has advised women to "Fake it until you can make it." But if you read this quote and applied it, could you be duped by someone applying Hillary's maxim? Not so easily. Faking it is only half of the answer to Brice's question. The other half is found in the fact that "rich and famous men" tend to be thoughtless concerning the woman's response.

Asking Hemingway's question to his female companion, in *For Whom the Bell Tolls*: "Did the earth move for you?" demonstrates a too little and too late concern for what *your* lover has been feeling. Here, sex is really a solo performance times two. If it were really a duet you would know without asking.[1]

But there is another question that needs answering, and that is what motivates women to fake it? Frigid women tend to pursue rich and famous men more single-mindedly than do sexually responsive women. Why is this the case? Two reasons suggest themselves. First, sensing they have less to offer in love and affection, they realize they must counter this deficiency with greater effort in the male's career pursuit, and hence they are more thorough as well as aggressive.

Somewhat confirming this conclusion, a British study, reported in the *Financial Times* (March 4, 2008), previously mentioned, reveals that a surprising 60 percent of British women would entertain a proposal to marry mainly for money. And if the women interviewed were over thirty years of age, the number would increase to 70 percent. Perhaps, if they would marry mainly for money, if they are willing to promise to "love, honor, and obey," mainly for money, they will not hesitate to throw in a fake orgasm. Notice also that this 60-70 percent is approximately the same number who do not consistently have an orgasm.[2]

On the other side of the net, with this common strategy of "faking it" to deal with, it becomes very important for men to be able to separate the genuine response from the fictitious. To be able to spot the symptoms of a nonorgasmic woman is one of the most important tasks a single man looking for a companion faces. Actresses (professional or amateur) are proof of the wisdom of SA'DI's observation that "Much contention and strife will arise in that house where the wife shall get up dissatisfied with her husband."[3]

But what is the cause of this dissatisfaction? Were these male victims of female frigidity themselves the cause of their wife's dysfunction? Was male clumsiness the reason? Obviously females would have it so. But scholarly research on the subject tends strongly to point in the other direction. It indicates that women who have never had an orgasm have often experimented with a multitude of men, with widely different attractions and techniques without any difference in outcome.

Let us look at the case of Pablo Picasso with Francois Gilot. We have already documented his comment that she was rather cold sexually. How did this relationship develop? She came to his studio for lessons in art and made herself useful around his studio and this soon developed an intimacy between them. While he was amused to have an admiring neophyte around to whom he could explain various aspects of his art, for her, the relationship gradually became more and more oppressive, with the result that after ten years, she vacated. She wrote a book of her experiences with Picasso to make a name for herself with an imitative art form.

We could repeat this plot with several other artists and their subsequent intimacies. So frequent in fact is this paradigm, it becomes a Hollywood plot form, as seen in the film *New York Stories*,[4] where the artist, played by Nick Nolte, convinces his ex-lover, played by Rosanna Arquette, that he needs her continued help in the studio and that he will no longer demand sex in exchange for her company. She soon goes out with another artist and the relationship with the character played by Nolte ends. Just to show the repetitive nature of these encounters, at the end of the film another aspiring artist flustered and excited at meeting Nolte, expresses herself as ready to fit into his established needs. Thus the merry-go-round recommences with the next artist and student admirer.

What we see in these situations is how young, good-looking and needy females throw themselves to the apparent generosity of older and successful artists. This is one of the ways that artists are induced into entering relationships with aspiring artists. How do rich and famous men end up with frigid women? This is one of many much-used ways.

(e) Sexual Differences

Take the seemingly bizarre story: a man leaves the house to go to the store for a loaf of bread, tea and cream, and he simply never returns to his home. Certainly we have heard such a story at least two or three times in our lives. It is generally rather amusing. Someone may ask: Did his wife ever hear from him again? Possibly not, comes the answer, usually with a half-concealed smile. It is not difficult to imagine follow-up questions: What about his former residence? His former work? His former friends? It is somewhat amusing—if you are not involved.

But let the same story be told of a woman and now a completely different mood and set of questions arise. Where did she finally turn up? Who was the last person she was last seen with? And the final question is the main one: who did she take off with?

Why this vast difference in response to these circumstances? The same scenario generically, but a completely different response.

A simple example, no doubt, but it points to a significant difference between men and women. Women are vastly more sociable than men. They develop facility with language up to a year earlier than the opposite sex, it appears. And this language difference, this advantage of women over men, continues, according to Nancy Fugate Woods, referred to earlier, until about the tenth year, when boys tend to catch up. (p. 34)[1]

Woods notices in passing that boys appear to be "more proficient at spatial and analytic abilities." But that is the end of the comparison. It appears that boys have a disadvantage that they eventually overcome. But if this basic difference between the sexes, as stated by Woods, were given the elaboration it deserves, it might begin another treatise on differences between male and female sexuality and intellects.

This treatise would being *in ventra sa mere* where the differences between the sexes are already apparent in the activity of the unborn.[2] Boys are much more active. They kick more, and require more frequent rest stops by pregnant women. Newborn females are quieter and stay closer to mom. They are better listeners, but less occupied with the external world. They learn language earlier, as Nancy Fugate Woods notices.

But what Woods does not especially notice, is what boys are doing while girls are occupying themselves with language. They are not idle, as one might imagine, they are more active in the real world of here and now. In the world of how things are moved by gravity, how they are pushed and pulled, how missiles and projectiles become airborne, land and explode, the strengths and weaknesses of boys and men, and their comparative fitness, speed, and agility. Activities in the here and now, as against the female attention to language, grammar and syntax—skills which are mostly useful in relation to yesterday and tomorrow, but not to the here and now of today.

In school, of course, it is language that counts, and not physical skills, which interest boys. The ability to listen and repeat what you have been told is what matters most. Hence girls are better in school, particularly in the lower grades where memory is the primary skill regarded. What is not realized is that memory, particularly memory for words and stories, is entirely passive. It produces nothing and invents nothing at that stage.

Creative invention is not a product of verbal skills. Verbal skills are a method for communication, but before you can communicate anything, you must have something to communicate, and finding that something is the product of preverbal skills of moving images in productive ways. To be sure, this is the theory of Albert Einstein, for whom moving images came first, and only when these images were developed into a coherent theory did he attempt to translate into language.

In his own words:

"The words or the language, as they are written or spoken, do not seem to play any role in my mechanism of thought. The physical entities which seem to serve as elements in thought are certain signs and more or less clear images which can be "voluntarily" reproduced and combined."

"The combinatory play seems to be the essential feature in productive thought—before there is any connection with logical construction in words or other kinds of signs which can be communicated to others."

"The above-mentioned elements are, in my case, of visual and some of muscular type. Conventional words of other signs have to be sought for laboriously. Only in a secondary stage, when the mentioned associative play is sufficiently established and can be reproduced at will."

"It seems to me that what you call full consciousness is a limited case which can never be fully accomplished. This seems to me connected with the fact called the narrowness of consciousness (*Enge des Bewusstseins*)."

Testimonial for an Essay on the Psychology of Invention in the Mathematical Field[3]

Images first, language afterward, in Einstein's account of his physical theories. From this account we construe that while girls were learning grammar, spelling and word fluency, boys were developing their relation to the world, as it exists here and now, and not in the realm of stories or plots which depend on language.

We might contrast the girls' superiority in language and grammatical fluency with boys' acquaintance with the immediate world as a gravitational familiarity with that world. The one seeks to achieve a linguistic familiarity, with various plot forms, which may be imposed on existence. The second seeks to learn the perimeters of various movements, which nature imposes on the human species.

The basic difference here is between language and images as methods for dealing with the problems of experience. Images have been given a superior role in this endeavor by the Einstein quotation. But language comes to the fore in social problems and solutions, which we experience with one another.

Thus we find that experience in dealing with medical problems and treatment, largely with the elderly, language and communication are of essential use in the survival of such patients. Indeed Harvard medical research has demonstrated that "people treated by a female doctor had a 4 percent lower relative risk of dying and 5 percent lower relative risk of being admitted to the hospital again in the following month," yielding 32,000 fewer deaths per year in the United States than by male doctors.[4]

What produced this significant differential between female doctors and male doctors? The answer is a concern for the patient as an individual whose needs and desires are a necessary part of a treatment, bringing a longer life to the patient and not merely, as in the case with a large percentage of male doctors, a generic labeling of illness. We should therefore notice that distinctions and valuations with a scientific basis, propounded by Einstein, may not be the only thing to consider. A method that saves 32,000 lives a year, is an achievement deserving of emphasis and applause.

(f) Images before Words

Pursuing Einstein's reported method of physical discovery or invention, we might consider what a profound difference it makes in our whole idea of invention or discovery, and the role of language in that activity. For the difference between images and words are not differences on an equal plane of usefulness, as commonly asserted. Something must come before words, or there would be no way of choosing one word over another.

Images come before words, and in their translation from images to words, words greatly reduce the size, scope, depth and variety of possible images to a communicable measure. Consider, for example, where you are now. Look around you, and attempt to frame in words an impression of what you see. Unless you are in a bare room—with no windows—you could work on the problem for the next day, week, or month, without succeeding.

There is a saying, "A picture is worth a thousand words."[1] We are inclined to regard the saying as hyperbole. But it is far from hyperbole; it is closer to hypo-bole—or understatement. Working with images, as Einstein did, before translation, is working in an infinitely richer environment than working in a verbal environment.[2]

What is lost in translation is the continuous wonder of an indeterminate reality. Aristotle says that philosophy began with a sense of wonder. That is also where it should end. For given the little we know about nature, our wonder should never cease. But it should not end as empty wonder. For nature exhibits tendencies which can be estimated, if not positively known. Indeed, science is built upon estimates of such tendencies.

This difference must be stressed because verbal fluency has been elevated to a position where it is considered the virtual essence of learning and intelligence. A quotation from past columnist William F. Buckley gives some idea of this distorted picture. "It was his conceit that if you couldn't write, you couldn't think; and that if you couldn't think, you were unlikely to prosper in his friendship."[3]

Possibly Buckley was being somewhat flip in this statement. But his interviews, on television, contain many excesses as silly as this quotation. In general, it is not only Buckley, but most well-known philosophers who regard language facility as equivalent to intelligence.

Another example possibly more serious from Victor Navasky writing in the *New York Times*, "Why Are Political Cartoons Incendiary?" "I have long had a theory that one reason people become as agitated by cartoons [illustrated by Daumier's cartoon of a giant Louis XIV swallowing everything mere mortals unload into his waiting mouth] is that there is no way of answering back" he finds. Navasky continues, "These days, neuroscientists tell us that if we want to understand our emotional reaction to what we see, we have to understand the brain, its right (emotional) and left (rational) spheres, and how the visual stimulus passes on information to the region called the amygdala, the brain's so-called fear center."[4]

Better than Buckley, no doubt, but only a distorted beginning, with this nonsense of emotional and rational centers. Ask what makes the rational center rational with nothing definite in sight. The point is that what we see—as an image—is closer to pictorial reality, even if it is distorted in the shape of a cartoon. On the other hand, what we hear are words, totally and deliberately fashioned into pragmatic plots to suit the intention and purpose of the speaker, as well as the reception of the hearer. The first introduces the possibility of distortion; the second guarantees it. There are no disinterested words.

This visual world is the world boys inhabit while girls are preoccupied with words—proper grammar, spelling and word fluency. With boys concerned with the manipulation of visual images, and girls with proper word order, the overwhelming advantage is not with the girls, as Nancy Fugate Woods appears to believe. It is with the boys, since it is with the manipulation of images and not with proper word order, that contact with reality begins, and from which all great inventions flow. Girls may have an advantage with "grammar, spelling, and word fluency," according to Nancy Fugate Woods, but this is a minor advantage next to what has been sacrificed to achieve it.

For what has been sacrificed is knowledge of how things—things in the environment—respond to touch, to gravity, and to being pushed, lifted and thrown in a variety of ways, in a variety of situations. Everything we have in common with the animal kingdom, in short, is sacrificed in the dubious interest of facility with words.

The point should be made, however, and should be made emphatically: Images are architectonic, words are subservient to images. This is a natural fact. And this natural fact points to another natural fact: that a boy's superior knowledge of moving images versus girl's superiority in language should not be encouraged in schools if we are seeking equal or more nearly equal outcomes from our educational systems.

For this dichotomy of images or words encourages a female dependency on the social milieu—from which grammar, spelling and word fluency emerge—while at the same time encouraging the relative independence of males from the same milieu. Thus, the manipulation of images is independent of any particular language. These are natural differences that eventually express themselves in the realm of sex.

(g) Social Assumptions/Natural Perceptions

Despite such differences, obvious differences, which are continuously ignored or minimized, men and women both tend to assume that members of the opposite sex are more like themselves than they really are. For educational places the sine qua non of intelligence is literacy. But if, on the other hand, intelligence is linked to invention, it becomes just as obvious that invention is not to be found in literature or literary skills, which is to say, not in words.

In the course of a normal day and night, for example, ask yourself how many activities require any kind of literacy to perform them? To go to the bathroom, to close or open windows, to straighten out the covers, in the wee hours of the morning, do you talk about the route to take, what you will wear or how you look? Or, take for example, you are driving to work and a car suddenly runs a stop street in your path, do you say "There's a car in my path, what should I do, put on the brakes or try to go around?" by which time you will have crashed into the car. Absolutely without words you decide whether to brake or swerve, or do both of these things.

Einstein's summary of his method dealt with similar, If much deeper questions. Scientific theories, at least his own, are not formulated or dependent on words for their invention, but on images being moved in various ways in space. And only when the theory reached the point of conviction did he attempt to translate these images into language or languages. It is also important to note that the theories in question were non-semantic until this time when a language or languages had to be selected for it's communication.

But to return to our more mundane or prosaic examples, some people will doubtless say that they do talk to themselves continuously. At least the possibility recently occurred to me, when, in a store, I heard an elderly couple admit that they characteristically talked to themselves more or less without end.

But not about brushing our teeth in the morning, we should interject, even here, some topics must be pre-semantic. So also, getting dressed, eating breakfast, backing one's vehicle out of the garage, and so forth. How much of this primary activity do we explain to others or ourselves in linguistic terms? We move without words, intelligently, rationally, but like the rest of the animal kingdom we inhabit, we move prelinguistically.

Words are used for communication, not primarily for first hand invention, or theorizing, as it is so frequently and continuously assumed (particularly in schools). But in schools, bureaucracy has its purpose: if they did not deal with words, they would have to deal with things or actions: a much more demanding if inventive activity.

In any case, in long marriages, it is sometimes quite surprising to find the shock of participants to learn that their lifelong partner views things quite differently from themselves. Where have they been all this time? Participants may wonder aloud. What have they been doing? Have we not discussed these things?—one or both of the partners may question. It seems that marital discussions frequently have not been dialogues, but take the form of parallel monologues.

It points to the fact that over and above conversations—in words, let us not forget—sympathy is not basically semantic. It may be emotional; it may be tactile; it may be olfactory; it may be sexual. It points to the fact that long-term relationships between a man and a woman depend not on intellectual agreement, but on a physical or sexual sympathy.

Earlier I described in general terms what I conceived to be the best possible relationship for a man and a woman. I described it as one where the male or husband is not only a lover, but a father and brother to his wife, and she, on her part, is a lover, mother and sister to him. At least, this in lieu of a now traditional, if antiquated relationship in which the families of both bride and groom not only come together for the wedding, but stay together in the marriage which followed. (as we have previously described)

Let us recall in Pietro Germi's _Divorce Italian Style_ (1961) [1], our hero, Marcello Mastroianni is taken with his cousin, the beautiful Stefania Sandrelli, and he can only see his way to satisfy his errant desire by marrying her. But alas, he is already married and divorce was illegal in Italy at the time. So he conceives a plot: a local priest's godson is left alone with his wife, with whom Mastroianni no longer has relations. An affair develops between the godson and Mastroianni's wife. Complications develop, and the godson is shot and killed by his own wife for philandering. Satisfying an option as it existed under the criminal code in Italy at that time, Mastroianni then shoots his wife, and in court pleads a crime of passion. He is soon back with his extended family, where he marries his beautiful cousin. The last scene finds them on a boat with a sailor attending to the cruise. While Mastroianni is romanticizing his newly wedded-wife in a face-to-face posture, out of sight, she is tickling the sailor with her extended foot.

Here we have a popular drama that was based on the insane prohibitions and strictures of the now outmoded Italian society. Thus natural perceptions have been rescheduled to fit the outmoded schemes and customs of the social order.

CHAPTER 7
Albert Einstein's Invention

This essay began in a somewhat comic vein with a reference to a *New York Times* article which featured an even three-way division between sexual responsiveness of women in the United States—one-third orgasmic, one-third nonorgasmic, one-third sometimes orgasmic. Of course such a division could hardly be maintained, much less ever reached, but the neat geometry caused me to think more seriously about the problem of orgasm in women; that together with my own divorce and the problem of finding an orgasmic woman, free and in my age-range, caused me to see this it as a real problem. Forty percent of marriages are remarriages, and when we consider that 80 percent of divorces list sexual incompatibility as a cause, the problem is staggering.[1]

One of the main objects of this essay is to provide an answer to the question of "Why so many rich and famous men often marry frigid women"—according to the question proposed by famed *Ziegfeld Follies's* Fanny Brice. Her answer is because they are such actresses."[2]

Indeed, the depth of the problem is well illustrated when we consider that three of the sexiest women in Hollywood past were nonorgasmic. These women, discussed in this book, Rita Hayworth, Ava Gardner, and Marilyn Monroe all illustrate this problem. Marilyn Monroe frankly admits it; Ava Gardner's remarks make that inference unavoidable. Rita Hayworth's alcoholism, physical aggression and five marriages permit little doubt. Love goddesses they were called. No-love goddesses would have been more accurate.

The problem of female orgasm is nothing new. It is found as early as the drama in Euripides's *Medea* from the fourth century BCE.[3] Publishers and producers today bite their tongue in mentioning the topic. Why? Because they do not wish to alienate a large portion of film patrons, one might assume. Thus Hollywood has been motivated to avoid the problem. A nonorgasmic woman cannot be ridiculed, and the nonresponsive woman is never the cause of a philandering companion, according to Hollywood doctrine

Then Christianity in the year 1309 mandated sinful sex as an article of faith. Henceforth one was not supposed to enjoy sex. Sex was for the purpose of producing children.[4]

Indeed Christianity brought with it a complete revolution in civilized values between Aristotle's *Ethics*, which considered how a man should act, and St. Augustine's *Confessions*, which considered what a man should avoid. Principally on this basis the philosopher Frederick Nietzsche, declared Christianity to be a feminine enterprise.[5-7]

In chapter 4, we counter the advice made popular by Hillary Clinton, as publicized by Maureen Dowd in the *New York Times*, "Fake it until you can make it," which adopted, at least some of the time by 50 percent of American women, cast a shroud over the problem. How to pull the shroud down and expose the problem is the subject matter of chapter 5.[8]

How can a man avoid the fate Fanny Brice envisions for him, we should question. By becoming conscious of the problem as presented here. Second is by recognizing certain unavoidable external signs given by a nonorgasmic woman. These signs are discussed in the fifth chapter of this book; ten external signs are considered. In short, the aim of this book is to equip a man with the means to identify and avoid the grasp of the nonorgasmic woman. And to avoid in the process the fate of men like Ernest Hemingway (who rumor has it, never had sex with his fourth wife), as well as Pablo Picasso (who told Françoise Gilot she was too cool).[9] Or President John F. Kennedy (whose father-in-law told his daughter Jacqueline that as soon as a woman gives in to a man, she will lower herself in his estimate).[10]

These men found themselves unhappy with frigid woman to begin with. This might have been avoided if they knew the signs of a nonorgasmic woman. Briefly recapped, the signs:

First, women twice-divorced. I say almost, because someone like Richard Burton's statements about Elizabeth Taylor and her passion is too convincing to ignore. Apart from a few isolated testimonies such as this, the majority of double divorcees confirm this fact.[11]

Second are workaholics. This term can be applied to women who have substituted some other activity for sex. Why should she do this? Because early training has placed high praise of such a substitution, and it would require analysis to remove this distortion.

The "control-freak" is a third sign of misplaced sexuality. As Freud theorized, there is little doubt that extreme behavior is caused by marred sexuality. Where one is taught to say no from an early age—it is virtually impossible to change.

The fourth symptom is "pitch and switch." It is a kind of halfway house between no and yes. Or at least the woman thinks it is. Perhaps the thought is more along the lines of, "If only the right man would come along." But she is confused as to where the problem lies. There is no right man. The problem is incapacity to let go. The enthusiasm is forced when she promotes sexuality, but indifference grows until habitually settling into gradual negativity.

The fifth symptom, "hyper indecision." To pick up our story of Jacqueline Kennedy's confession that her most grievous fault was her inability to sustain an initial enthusiasm—invites Freudian analysis and the suggestion that it all stems from continued pull in mental distress.

The sixth indication of frigidity is the condition of doing "nothing in moderation." An example of this is women who are spendthrifts: Jacqueline Kennedy's continuous spending on clothes. This spending was another case of substituted satisfactions and can often be seen on an elaborate scale.

The seventh and eighth questions we should ask to potential companions are the issues of delinquent dads and mindful. Unhappy parents create children who replicate their parents' maladjusted behavior. As an example, Hillary Clinton exemplified this condition—she could never get her father's attention or approval.[12] She disagreed with her husband Bill, when he was Governor of Arkansas, according to complaints of neighbors. (Their marriage was a replication of her parent's unhappy marriage. This is why a study of the family situation must be a requirement for a full understanding of the preferences and prejudices of the female in question.)

Ninth sign can be found in the expression: "Let's be friends." This statement could mean a variety of things that we have already surveyed. The point is to see it as a plea for a non-sexual relation and to act accordingly.

Tenth, Post-Coitum. Eventually, the acting breaks down. For those faking it do not realize that a good orgasm generates a good mood. The fact is that how soon and where arguments start after sex is an indicator of no female orgasm. This is where the acting falls flat.

One should keep these clues or symptoms nearby, as the irascible need a female may exhibit may not be what it seems, instead it could be a deep and constant reaction to being an unwilling spectator to male sexual satisfaction. Knowing this difference is the first step to knowing what to do about it. One should move to the broadest implication of this taxonomy, which leave one-third of women in the United States as unwilling participants in a physiological drama which demands their participation, but which is to them, meaningless and painful.

"What about men?" A woman might well ask. In the present day, with the differences between men and women narrowing, we should attempt to recover biological differences to adjust this imbalance. I am the father of a boy and a girl. We knew several months before the birth of the second child that it was a boy. Their mother would awake in the middle of the night due to his kicking.

No such inquiry was apparent with the first child, who was a girl. The activity of the male was caused by the addition of the Y chromosome to his physiognomy. Announcing the sexual fact, the male in the womb is more aggressive and demonstrative than the female. But on the other hand, female infants and toddlers are ahead of males in grammar by several years. So much so that teachers often wish to hold boys back until they catch up. The idea shows the tunnel vision that mainstream education has. All they need to do is ask, what are the boys doing while the girls are studying grammar?

Once the question is asked the answer becomes obvious—they are studying gravity. This means walking, running, jumping, fighting, wrestling, bats and balls, how things stand and fall, and so on. The discoveries that boys often make are a matter of the movement of things in the environment. Educators might ask what good are grammatical studies opposed to gravitational studies for a successful life—where success is not defined by repetition and memory but by unique innovations. The national norm for testing high-school students in the United States is based on memory, not innovation.

Authority for this approach might be found in Albert Einstein's statement that language figured very little in his discovery of the theory of relativity. It was only after his first discovery of specific relativity that he needed to translate into a common language. We might generalize Einstein's statement to conclude that language is not the tool of invention but a means of communication once a new theory is found. The great mistake of modern education is to think otherwise.[14]

Part of the reason for this is the mistake of educators who assume (what is convenient) that students sitting still are ready to learn. Sitting quietly in one's seat is the next thing to not being there at all. The fact is that students who are active are better learners than those who are passive. This lesson has been taken to heart by the country of Finland, which has structured their school day with an hour of class divided into thirty-five minutes of classroom instruction, followed by twenty-five minutes of outdoor activities. Studies of active gravity should have precedence; passive education of grammar should be tagged as a memorial method, not for discovery.

In any case, because school is largely memory-based, apart from art, film, television, computer production and shop classes, success is a matter of protocol with little thinking involved. It does not promote later success where innovation is required, but it continues with initial preferences that were exhibited in the first years of life on this planet. Thus in reading the newspaper, males read sports, while females study the style section. And males are aggressive in social and sexual relations, which results in a strange imbalance. Males are instructed to pursue females; females are instructed to say no to intimate relations. The result of saying no for many years becomes for many females an irreversible habit whereby it becomes almost impossible to say yes. Thus the problem arises. Out of more than four thousand animal species, less than a handful are monogamous. Therefore the social structure produces the problem of nonorgasmic women.[15] It is nurture not nature largely perpetuating this problem.

EPILOGUE
Freud vs Reich on Sublimation

We have covered the experiences that have resulted in a large percentage of modern women becoming nonorgasmic. But to see the picture in its most meaningful terms we must turn from the micro-math to the macro. By this I mean national numbers and similar causes.

Sigmund Freud and Wilhelm Reich agree about one very important concept in psychoanalysis. They agree that modern civilization was built on the concept of sublimation but they disagreed on its alleged significance or necessity. [1] Freud argues that the trade-off of sex for financial success and for the promotion of civilization is a necessary condition of that success. Wilhelm Reich in his response argued that it is an aberration to sacrifice sex for business or career success. He questioned why anyone would give up one of the main rewards of an activity in order to finance its achievement. [2]

The banishment of Wilhelm Reich from the Freudian Canon—and the burning of his books (yes, they burned his books!)—indicates the continued existence of shockingly repressive elements in the society. Who is Wilhelm Reich, you may ask. To this question you would be hard pressed to get a clear-cut answer, since his banishment from the Freudian canon resulted in his banishment from the media as well. To volunteer a cameo, he is sometimes outed as a spiritual contributor to the Esalen Institute in Big Sur, on the California coast.

Reich made orgasm the vital center of his psychological analysis. In his theory, orgasm was the emotional energy regulator of the body, whose function was to dissipate sexual tensions. If orgasm was not experienced in intercourse, or if orgasm was not equal in strength to the individual's sexual tensions, emotional energy was expressed through nonsexual and neurotic channels, Reich theorized.

So far, so good, one might think. But Reich apparently went too far, and he wound up jailed for fraud and misrepresentation. Naturally, with this public stigma—and no sufficiently loud defense—he was eliminated from respectable psychoanalysis and from media coverage. Unfortunately this elimination meant not only eliminating his excesses—if such they were—but of the centrality of orgasm from the Freudian Canon.

Thus, for example, one notes the absence of orgasm from the topics treated in Dr. Robert M. Goldenson's *The Encyclopedia of Human Behaviuor*.[3] Reich is dismissed as a quack whose "fanciful" theories failed to take into account the "well-known" fact "that many highly disturbed individuals are capable of full orgastic potency."

In fact, Reich never claimed that disturbed individuals are incapable of orgasm. His argument ran in the other direction: his claim being that individuals who did not experience orgasm exhibited neurotic anxieties—not the reverse, not that one could not experience orgasm if one was neurotic. In any case, potency is defined as potential and not performance, and Reich was concerned with converting the former—potential—into performance. No, Reich's offense was more basic. He went further than anyone else to disturb the democratic apple cart of equal sexual opportunity. The reason doesn't matter.

In 2010 Christopher Ryan and Cacilda Jetha in their *Sex at Dawn: The Prehistoric Origins of Modern Sexuality* write that sex, as we know it today is not "natural."[4] In fact, monogamy did not come into existence until the invention of agriculture, before which societies were far more egalitarian and open to sexuality than we are today. With the rise of agriculture comes the institution of class societies, and with class societies comes the repression of sexuality.

But of course, repression of sexuality means heterosexual coupling, not the "message" practiced by doctors to relieve—by orgasm—symptoms of hysteria, such as "anxiety, sleeplessness, irritability, nervousness" and "erotic fantasies," which were, in the late nineteenth century, "the largest single market for therapeutic services."

Accordingly, debunked by Ryan and Jetha, is the somewhat popular notion that women are naturally less sexual than men. And with it the *New York Times* one-third, one-third, one-third taxonomy with which we began. This, it now clearly appears, is not biological or natural, but conditioned by the class structure of society. It is a position which Wilhelm Reich would embrace.[5]

We must look elsewhere for a good balance between the realization of sex and the rewards of a well-balanced society. Suffice to say, Hillary Clinton's maxim: "Fake it until you can make it," in practice, becomes simply "Fake it!" Sigmund Freud theorized that we "sublimate" our sex drive in order to achieve financial and career success. What he did not remark, to my knowledge, is that this sublimation frequently destroys the sex-drive it sets out to satisfy, and the marriage it was sacrificed to promote. To paraphrase and supplement Jacqueline Kennedy's father: "It's either a happy sex life and marriage, or financial and career success: they rarely go together."[6]

Hong Kong, according to University of Chicago Economist Milton Friedman, produced the most perfect form of a competitive economic system in the world.[7] It also produced the society with the smallest number of orgasmic women: nineteen percent, one remembers. The lesson should be clear: the stiffest competition also produces the most flaccid sexuality. Professor Friedman neglected to point this out.[8]

Of course his defenders might assert that corollaries are not proof. Yet if we look at the other side of the globe, we find the exact opposite: one of the weakest economies produced the highest number of orgasmic women—91 percent orgasmic in Italy. An accident? The relation of sexuality to economics is consistent. We have commented that almost one hundred years ago this relation was discussed by psychoanalyst Sigmund Freud. He called the relation between career and sexuality sublimation, and he explained that modern societies are built on the capacity—one might call it a gradual and great error—of redirecting the sex drive into business competition for the social power it yields. But Freud failed to notice the loss this substitution invariably involved. In part, this failure is the result of keeping a different consequence in different disciplines and separate compartments—economics on the one hand and sexual psychology on the other—leading to a social blindness as to their actual connection.

One more example may be necessary to convincing doubters—one which involves a total rejection of the modern competitive model, such as we have seen in Polynesia, where modern economic competition was reduced if not absent. Here we find something like 100 percent of women experience orgasm. One might call this fact more or less conclusive proof of the eventual effects of Freud's theory of sublimation.

In other words, urging what world statistics demonstrate, contrary to popular opinion, that financial and sexual success are inversely related to one another, in such a way that as one gains financial success, sexual success is lost. Thus, to repeat for the last time Fanny Brice's crucial question: "Why do so many rich and famous men wind up with frigid women?" Our final answer is: to be rich and famous in modern society means exactly the opposite of what entrepreneurs think it means—wholly or partially abandoning one's claim to successful sexual relations.

Great success in finance, business and career all tend very strongly to result in preventing success in sexual relations. The unsuccessful marriages of Franklin Roosevelt, Joseph Kennedy and sons, and Bill Clinton—for glaring examples—are not unusual in this respect. They represent the trade-off one must make: public success, private failure. They represent the American paradigm. This is the down side of sex in America, promoted or copied elsewhere in the so-called modern world.

NOTES

Chapter 1

1. *The New York Times* (2005).

   Also stated: *Wikipedia* (Female Sexual Dysfunction): "About one-third of the women experienced sexual dysfunction."

   Wikipedia (Orgasm Disorders): "Absence of orgasm following a normal sexual excitement phase in at least 75 percent of sexual encounters."

2. Frank Harris, *My Life and Loves* (Paris, the author [priv. print.] 1922).

Chapter 2

1. *The Bribe* (film, distributed: Metro-Goldwyn-Mayer, 1949).

2. Lee Server, *Love is Nothing* (First St. Martin's, 2006).

3. Ava Gardner, *Ava: My Story* (Bantam, 1990).

4. *The Sun Also Rises* (film, distributed: 20th Century Fox, 1957).

5. Ernest Hemingway, *A Farewell to Arms* (Scribner, 1929).

6. Ernest Hemingway, *For Whom the Bell Tolls* (Scribner, 1940).

7.   Jane Ridley, "Fake It Until You Can Make It," *New York Daily News*, September 28, 2006.

"Women rarely admit to faking, even to their friends after a bottle or two of wine. But a recent online survey by Redbook magazine found 52% of American women frequently pretend they've climaxed."

Also stated: Brian Alexander, "Sorry, Guys: Up to 80 Percent of Women Admit Faking It," *NBCNews.com*, June 30, 2016.

Also stated: *Brewer's Survey*: "25% [of women] used vocalization to fake orgasm in 90% of the instances that they would not reach climax."

8.   Stanley Bernard Frank, *The Sexually Active Man Past Forty* (Macmillan, 1968).

Chapter 3

1.   Euripides, *Medea* (431 BC), trans. Rex Warner (Dover Thrift Editions, Editor: Stanley Appelbaum).

2.   Sadi, *Gulistan or Flower-Garden* (1258 AD), trans. James Ross (The Walter Scott Publishing Company, 1894).

3.   "The Seven Spiritual Ages of Mrs. Marmaduke Moore," poem by Ogden Nash (1933).

4.   Maureen Dowd, "An Ideal Husband," *New York Times*, July 6, 2008.

5. Dale Carnegie, *How to Win Friends and Influence People* (Simon and Schuster, 1936).

6. Aristotle, *Nicomachean Ethics* (350 B.C.E), trans. W.D. Ross (The Internet Classics Archive).

    Book II: The virtues of character can be found as means.

7. Marilyn Yalom, "How the French Invented Love," *The Wall Street Journal*, October 20–21, 2012.

Chapter 4

1. Maureen Dowd, "Fake It Until You Can Make It," *New York Times*, June 8, 2012.

2. Jane Ridley, "Fake It Until You Can Make It," *New York Daily News*, September 28, 2006.

3. Barbara Walters, *Audition: A Memoir, How to Talk with Practically Anybody About Practically Anything* (Knopf, 2008).

Chapter 5

Section (i)

1. *Financial Times*, March 4, 2008.

2. Jane Ridley, "Fake It Until You Can Make It," *New York Daily News*, September 28, 2006.

Section (ii)

1. Barbara Walters, *Audition: A Memoir, How to Talk with Practically Anybody About Practically Anything* (Knopf, 2008).

Section (iii)

1. *Seven Beauties* (film, director: Lina Wertmuller, produced: Medusa Distribuzione, 1975)

2. Carl Bernstein, *A Woman in Charge: The Life of Hillary Rodham Clinton* (Vintage Books, 2007).

Section (iv)

1. Marcel Proust, *Swann's Way, In Search of Lost Time* #1 (Grasset and Gallimard, 1913).

Section (v)

1. Phillip French, *The Observer*, "Screen Legends," (July 13, 2008).

2. Ernest Hemingway, *The Sun Also Rises* (Scribner, 1926).

3. *The Misfits* (film, director: John Huston, produced: Seven Arts Productions, 1961).

4. *The Manchurian Candidate* (film, director: John Frankenheimer, produced: George Axelrod, 1962)

5. Nicholas Fraser, Philip Jacobson, Mark Ottaway, and Lewis Chester, *Aristotle Onassis* (Lippincott, 1977).

Section (vi)

1. Aristotle, *Nicomachean Ethics* (350 B.C.E), trans. W.D. Ross (The Internet Classics Archive).

   Book III. Chapters 6–12, First examples of moral virtues

2. *The Man Who Loved Women* (film, director: Francois Truffaut, dis: United Artists, 1977).

3. Euripides, *Medea* (431 BC), trans. Rex Warner (Dover Thrift Editions, Editor: Stanley Appelbaum).

Section (vii)

1. *The Singing Detective* (British television series, created: Dennis Potter, BBC1, 1986).

Section (viii)

1. Hillary Clinton, *A Woman in Charge: The Life of Hillary Rodham Clinton* (Vintage Books, 2007).

2. Barbara Walters, *Audition: A Memoir, How to Talk with Practically Anybody About Practically Anything* (Knopf, 2008).

3. Maureen Dowd, "An Ideal Husband," *New York Times*, July 6, 2008.

Section (ix)

1. Democratic National Convention address, speech given by Bill Clinton (July 25, 2016).

Section (x)

1. "post coitum omne animal triste est, sive gallus et mulier:"

   trans: "After sex all animals are sad except the cock and the woman."

   Latin proverb originally attributed to Galen, a Greek physician (2nd century AD), he linked the four temperaments sanguine, phlegmatic, choleric and melancholic to bodily dispositions. Sometimes (without the cock/woman add-on) Aristoteles is named as the author.

2. Caroline Moorehead, *Gellhorn: A Twentieth-Century Life* (Macmillan, 2004).

3. *When Harry Met Sally* (dir: Rob Reiner, dis: MGM, 1989).

4. Charles Chaplin, *My Autobiography* (Melville House Books, 1964).

Chapter 6

(A) THE GREATEST PLEASURE OR WORST PAIN

1. Nancy Fugate Woods, "Human Sexuality in Health and Illness," *American Journal of Nursing* 76, no. 1 (1976): 79.

2. Mark Grief, "Still Superior," *London Review of Books* (February 12, 2009), Book review of *Reborn: Early Diaries 1947–1964*, by Susan Sontag, edited by David Rieff.

3. Naomi Wolf, *Vagina, A New Biography* (Ecco, 2012).

4. Zoe Heller, "Pride and Prejudice," *The New York Review of Books* (Vol. 59, Number 14; September 27, 2012), Book review of *Vagina, A New Biography*, by Naomi Wolf (Ecco, 2012).

(B) SEXUAL PROGRESS/REGRESS

1. Feifei Sun, "The Misconduct Matrix," *Time International (Atlantic Ed.)* 117, no. 22 (2011): 23.

2. Robert M. Goldenson, *The Encyclopedia of Human Behavior, Vol 1 & 2* (Doubleday and Company, 1970).

3. Christopher Ryan and Cacilda Jetha, *Sex at Dawn: The Prehistoric Origins of Modern Sexuality* (Harper Collins, 2010).

4. *The New York Times* (2005).

    Also stated: *Wikipedia.com* (Female Sexual Dysfunction): "About one-third of the women experienced sexual dysfunction."

    Wikipedia.com (Orgasm Disorders): "Absence of orgasm following a normal sexual excitement phase in at least 75 percent of sexual encounters."

5. Terry Tom Brown, "Love and Other Animals: To Black Vultures, Infidelity Doesn't Come without Consequence," *The Guardian Weekly*, September 8, 2012.

    Meg Barker, "So Monogamy Works for Some Animals: Doesn't Mean It's 'Natural' for Us," *The Guardian Weekly*, July 30, 2013.

(C) THE MISLEADING MEDIA

1. John Pilger, "Why Are Wars not Being Reported Honestly?," *The Guardian*, December 10, 2010.

2. Edward Bernays, *Propaganda* (Ig Publishing, 1928).

3. Feifei Sun, "The Misconduct Matrix," *Time International (Atlantic Ed.)* 117, no. 22 (2011): 23.

4. Nancy Fugate Woods, "Human Sexuality in Health and Illness," *American Journal of Nursing* 76, no. 1 (1976): 79.

5. Sam Kashner, "Marilyn and Her Monsters," *Vanity Fair*, November 2010.

6. Woods, "Human Sexuality in Health and Illness."

(D) WHY DO SO MANY RICH AND FAMOUS MEN...?

1. Ernest Hemingway, *For Whom the Bells Tolls* (Scribner, 1940).

2. *Financial Times*, March 4, 2008.

3. Sadi, *Gulistan or Flower-Garden* (1258 AD), trans. James Ross (The Walter Scott Publishing Company, 1894).

4. New York Stories (directors: Woody Allen, Francis Ford Coppola, Martin Scorsese, distributed Buena Vista Pictures, 1989).

(E) SEXUAL DIFFERENCES

1. Nancy Fugate Woods, "Human Sexuality in Health and Illness," *American Journal of Nursing* 76, no. 1 (1976): 79.

2. "En ventra sa mere"

   French phrase, trans: "In his/her mother's belly," refers to a "fetus in utero"

3. Albert Einstein, "A Mathematician's Mind," in *Ideas and Opinions* (Portland, OR: Broadway Books, 1995), 35–36.

   Jacques S. Hadamard, *Testimonial for an Essay on the Psychology of Invention in the Mathematical Field* (Princeton, NJ: Princeton University Press, 1945).

4. James Hamblin, "Evidence of the Superiority of Female Doctors" *The Atlantic*, Dec 19, 2016.

(F) IMAGES BEFORE WORDS

1. *Wikipedia.com* ("A picture is worth a thousand words")

   English idiom, first used by Tess Flanders (1911), British newspaper article: "Use a picture. It is worth a thousand words."

2. Albert Einstein, "A Mathematician's Mind," in *Ideas and Opinions* (Portland, OR: Broadway Books, 1995), 35–36.

Jacques S. Hadamard, *Testimonial for an Essay on the Psychology of Invention in the Mathematical Field* (Princeton, NJ: Princeton University Press, 1945).

3.   Neal B. Freeman, "Buckley, If Not God, Returns to Yale: What the Late, Great Controversialist Would Have Said to Mitt Romney, Rick Perry, and Today's Conservative Talking Heads," *The Wall Street Journal*, November 5–6, 2011.

4.   Victor Navasky, "Why Are Political Cartoons Incendiary?" *New York Times*, November 13, 2011.

(G) SOCIAL ASSUMPTIONS/NATURAL PERCEPTIONS

1.   *Divorce Italian Style* (Italian film, director: Pietro Germi, distributed Embassy Pictures, 1961).

2.   "Italy Divorce: Rate Continues to Increase," *Huffington Post, upi.com*, July 8, 2011, updated September 7, 2011.

"Rise in Italian divorces 0.2 percent."

Chapter 7

Footnote 1. *The New York Times* (2005).

Also stated in: *Wikipedia.com* (Female Sexual Dysfunction): "About one-third of the women experienced sexual dysfunction."

Wikipedia.com (Orgasm Disorders): "Absence of orgasm following a normal sexual excitement phase in at least 75 percent of sexual encounters."

2. *Biography.com* (Fanny Brice)

   "Men always fall for frigid women because they put on the best show."

3. Euripides, *Medea* (431 BC), trans. Rex Warner (Dover Thrift Editions, Editor: Stanley Appelbaum).

4. infoplease.com/encyclopedia (Roman Catholic Church History)

   "Avignon residence (1309–1378)—the so-called Babylonian captivity of the papacy, a time of good church administration, but of excessive French influence over papal policy."

5. Richard McKeon, ed., *Introduction to Aristotle*, Second edition revised and enlarged (The University of Chicago Press, Random House, 1947).

   "Ethics," 332–38.

6. St. Augustine, *Confessions* (397–400).

   Also referenced: William G. T. Shedd, ed., *Confessions of Augustine* (Andover, 1860).

7. Sander L. Gilman, Carole Blair, and David J. Parent, eds. and trans., *Friedrich Nietzsche on Rhetoric and Language* (Oxford University Press, 1989).

8. Maureen Dowd, "Fake It Until You Can Make It," *New York Times*, June 8, 2012.

9. Francoise Gilot, *Life with Picasso* (1964).

10. C. David Heymann, *A Woman Named Jackie: An Intimate Biography of Jacqueline Bouvier Kennedy Onassis* (Signet, 1990).

11. Chris Williams, *The Richard Burton Diaries* (Yale University Press, 2012).

12. Carl Bernstein, *A Woman in Charge: The Life of Hillary Rodham Clinton* (Vintage Books, 2007).

13. Albert Einstein, "A Mathematician's Mind," in *Ideas and Opinions* (Portland, OR: Broadway Books, 1995), 35–36.

    Jacques S. Hadamard, *Testimonial for an Essay on the Psychology of Invention in the Mathematical Field* (Princeton, NJ: Princeton University Press, 1945).

14. Terry Tom Brown, "Love and Other Animals: To Black Vultures, Infidelity Doesn't Come without Consequence," *The Guardian Weekly*, September 8, 2012.

    Also stated: Meg Barker, "So Monogamy Works for Some Animals: Doesn't Mean It's 'Natural' for Us," *The Guardian Weekly*, July 30, 2013.

Epilogue

1. Wilhelm Reich, *Ether, God and Devil/Comic Superimposition* (Farrar, Straus and Giroux, 1973).

    Also stated: Wilhelm Reich, *The Sexual Revolution* (Farrar, Straus and Giroux, 1973).

2. Reich, *The Sexual Revolution*.

3.   Robert M. Goldenson, *The Encyclopedia of Human Behavior, Vol 1 &
     2* (Doubleday and Company, 1970).

4.   Christopher Ryan and Cacilda Jetha, *Sex at Dawn: The Prehistoric
     Origins of Modern Sexuality* (Harper Collins, 2010).

5.   *The New York Times* (2005).

     Also stated: *Wikipedia.com* (Female Sexual Dysfunction): "About
     one-third of the women experienced sexual dysfunction."

     Wikipedia.com (Orgasm Disorders): "Absence of orgasm following
     a normal sexual excitement phase in at least 75 percent of sexual
     encounters."

6.   David Nasaw, *The Patriarch: The Remarkable Life and Turbulent
     Times of Joseph P. Kennedy* (Penguin Books, 2013).

7.   "End of an Experiment," *The Economist*, July 15, 2010.

     "[Hong Kong]...Milton Friedman once described as the world's
     greatest experiment in laissez-faire capitalism."

     Also stated: *Wikipedia.com* (Milton Friedman): "If you want to see
     capitalism in action, go to Hong Kong."

8.   *Wikipedia.com* (Human sexual activity).

     Also referencing: Sophie Mcintyre, "These Are the Most Sexually
     Satisfied Countries in the World," *indy100.independent.co.uk*.